# Synagogue Boards:
# A Sacred Trust

by Daniel S. Schechter

**UAHC**

UAHC Press
New York, New York

# To Sally

Library of Congress Cataloging-in-Publication Data

Schechter, Daniel S.
    Synagogue boards : a sacred trust / by Daniel S. Schechter.
        p. cm.
    Includes bibliographical references.
    ISBN 0-8074-0705-4 (alk. paper)
    1. Synagogue trustees. 2. Synagogues--Organization and administration. I. Title.

BM653 .S32 2000
296.6'5--dc21

                                      99-023111

# Acknowledgments

I need to express gratitude to many rabbis and teachers from all denominations who have helped me to grow Jewishly, but especially to my rabbi, Peter S. Knobel of Beth Emet The Free Synagogue in Evanston, Illinois. We share the belief that only through a collaborative relationship between clergy and volunteer leadership can synagogues become exciting communities which will be God-centered, text-centered, and ethics-centered. To Rabbi Dow Marmur of Holy Blossom Temple in Toronto, Ontario, goes my admiration for his clearly and beautifully written sermons, which have greatly influenced my thinking.

Thanks to Dr. Roberta Louis Goodman, R.J.E., for her chapter on Jewish education. Thanks also to Lawrence A. Sherman, a distinguished volunteer leader, for sharing his expertise on congregational budgeting. I would also like to thank the following for their contributions. Dr. Charles M. Olsen of the Heartland Presbyterian Center in Kansas City, Missouri, gave me permission to adapt the survey form created by the research services division of the Presbyterian Church (U.S.A.) for his pioneering project, "Lay Leaders Set Apart." Robert Mills, editor of the *Journal of the National Association of Temple Administrators*, for almost a decade gave me a platform for my "From the Boardroom" column. Dr. Robert Rotenberg of DePaul University, Chicago, developed the "Procedure for Self-Study of Congregational Worship," and the Central Conference of American Rabbis granted permission for its use as "Appendix E" of this book. Rabbi John S. Schechter of B'nai Israel Congregation in Basking Ridge, New Jersey, shares my fascination with issues of synagogue governance and was generous in offering his insightful comments and conversation-stopping questions.

Finally, I would like to express my appreciation to Kenneth Gesser, the publisher of the UAHC Press, who took a personal interest in the development of this book.

# Foreword

Synagogue trustees are expected not only to conserve the assets of the congregation but also to be leaders, to translate the needs of the congregation into goals, to initiate programs, and to plan effectively for the future. If ever there was an institution demanding dynamic volunteer leadership, it is the synagogue, which is in a state of continuing evolution as a center for Jewish communal life, Jewish education, social action, and social service. Still, above all, the synagogue is a worshiping community. To accomplish these and other important functions, trustees must also be concerned with establishing a sound organizational structure and fostering sound management.

What are the general functions of the board?

1. *To define the objectives of the synagogue, set goals, and approve policy for reaching these goals.* The board as a whole shares this responsibility with its committees and officers, and with the rabbis, cantor, administrator, and educator. But the board retains final accountability.

2. *To take action to reach its goals.* Good policy is without value unless supported by a good plan of implementation based on a sound financial structure.

3. *To define the roles of the top professionals.* It is the board's responsibility to find and install these leaders, to motivate and support them, and to evaluate, in an appropriate manner, their performance on a regular basis in the light of explicit position descriptions and mutually understood statements of expectations.

4. *To evaluate its own performance at regular intervals.* A high expectation of board members is that they will develop themselves Jewishly. Whether they have been brought up as Jews and attended religious school and synagogue services, or as adults have chosen to become Jews, trustees have a special responsibility to grow as Jews in order to perform effectively on the board. As Rabbi Lawrence Kushner of Congregation Beth El of the Sudbury River Valley, Massachusetts, has told his board: "The best rule of thumb I have ever been able to formulate was the 'one-third' rule. If you manage to see to it that one-third of the time you devote to the synagogue each week is devoted to your own personal growth (it could be prayer, it could be study, it could be acts of social justice, anything) then, not only will you continue growing as a Jew, but you will be a much more happy and effective leader."[1]

# Contents

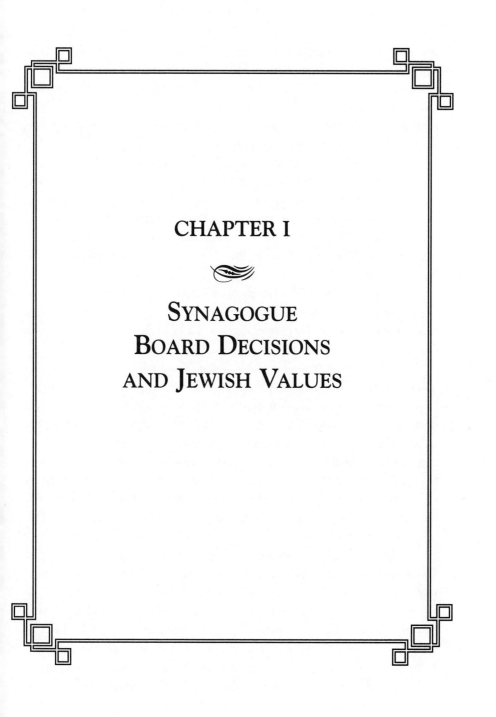

# CHAPTER I

# SYNAGOGUE BOARD DECISIONS AND JEWISH VALUES

Synagogue trustees are architects for change. Their challenge is to invent the future of the synagogue, in concert with the clergy, education director, and administrator. That is not accomplished in one brief moment of courageous commitment, but through heroic wrestling with daily obstacles. Lay leadership, who are closest to the feelings, needs, and concerns of the congregation, do not complete their job until the congregation has become a worshiping and learning community.

When Jews talk about the religious life of the congregation — its health as a worshiping community — we seldom think of the synagogue board. We think of the rabbi and the cantor, and we may think of the committee variously known as worship, ritual, or religious practices. But we do not think about the board of trustees, the highest policy-making body in the congregation. That should not be the case, and in itself suggests that we have a problem.

If we are going to work toward becoming a holy people (*am kadosh*), we need to examine the roles of boards of trustees in every synagogue, because trustees are frequently the missing link in making decisions on the religious life of the community, including matters of worship.

Most synagogue trustees lack the Judaic knowledge to employ Jewish-value-based decision making, sometimes referred to as "Torah-based governance." The format and spirit of synagogue board meetings do not foster such an approach. However, it is only through education and actual practice in board meetings that trustees can be helped to understand themselves as a community of spiritual leaders. When professionals (rabbis, cantors, educators, and administrators) and volunteers have exhibited a partnership in leadership and a shared commitment to the content of Jewish life, such role modeling has had dramatic results in the quality of life of the synagogue. Lay empowerment represents the best hope for creating a community of knowledgeable and committed laity. The shared participation of open and learned clergy with serious Jewish laity offers the possibility of a transformative experience for individuals and institutions.

Dr. David Ellenson, professor at Hebrew Union College–Jewish Institute of Religion, laments that "the most significant division in the contemporary Jewish community is that between the minority of Jews for whom Judaism is at the center of their lives and the majority for whom it is peripheral at best."[1] Therein lies the challenge to synagogue trustees: to draw Judaism to the center of their own lives and to help their fellow congregants do the same. The role of lay leaders — like that of their rabbinic partners — is not to dictate religious behavior, but to inspire and support their community as people make difficult choices and commitments.

Jewish values should be at the heart of all congregational decisions. They are important to the synagogue as an institution, to its board of trustees, to each trustee, and to each Jew in his or her daily living — in the home and in the workplace, as well as in the boardroom. Jewish values are frequently derived by attempting to translate God's vision into human terms in the form of *mitzvot*, interpreted by some as commandments directly from God, while understood by others as the result of freely undertaken personal obligations.

It is important that boards understand the significance of what is Jewish in their heritage and of what Judaic values are at stake in their trusteeship. There are many examples of Judaic values key to synagogue decision making but frequently not recognized as being of Jewish heritage. I have selected a few as examples.

In Judaism the individual is defined in relationship to the Jewish community. It is as a community that we stand before God. One of the best-known statements in Jewish history is by Hillel: "If I am not for myself, who will be for me? And if I am only for myself, what am I?"(*Pirke Avot* 1:14)

Judaism places emphasis on a worshiping community and on making the congregation a caring community. It recognizes the importance of a financial commitment as well as a religious commitment. As it is written in *Pirke Avot*, the sayings of our ancestors, "*Ein kemach, ein Torah*": where there is no substance (generally thought of as money), there can be no study of Torah (*Pirke Avot* 3:17).

Rabbi Eric Yoffie, president of the Union of American Hebrew Congregations, observes that "Now more than ever we embrace ritual and prayer and ceremony; but like the prophets, we never forget that God is concerned about the everyday and that the blights of society take precedence over the mysteries of heaven. In these self-indulgent times, too many turn inward; but we know that there can be no Reform Judaism without moral indignation; and we know, too, that a Reform synagogue that does not alleviate the anguish of the suffering is a contradiction in terms."[2]

Synagogue trustees should, of course, concern themselves with making peace between board members or between others in the congregational family where there is potential strife. But, in addition, they should support the humane growth of the larger community by bringing Jews and non-Jews together for dialogue and for community action. Such positive social relations can lead to improvement in the overall quality of human life. While some trustees will be surprised at this being called a "Jewish" action, the lesson lies with the meaning of *tzedakah*, the Hebrew word denoting justice and righteousness. As Dr. Reuven Kimelman of Brandeis University has suggested, when a board acts in ways that do not immediately confer a financial advantage, it may be for a larger reason: "Judaism is the training ground for creating the consciousness of a mega-family which will incorporate all humanity."[3]

Judaism fosters the concept of the congregation as a "learning community," one that views all Jews, not just children, as potential learners, with learning as a lifetime pursuit. Such activities take place inside and especially outside the classroom and are grounded in significant Jewish experiences. Rabbi Yoffie called upon the 20,000 men and women on the boards of Reform synagogues to become "God wrestlers." Emphasizing that role models will forever be more powerful than Jewish ideology, he said that trustees "bear a heavy responsibility to preserve and transmit." How shall we begin? he asked rhetorically. Then he answered: "We shall begin with study of Torah."[4]

While our tradition, based on Torah and later interpretation, presents the imperative of quality, lifelong education for all Jews, how fully is this understood, funded, and implemented by synagogue boards? A new paradigm is needed for decision making in synagogues, combining elements of Jewish-value-based decision making with the exercise of governance on management issues. Questions that need to be addressed in the context of this new paradigm include:

• How well is the board serving the religious mission of the synagogue?

• To what extent would an increase in attention to religious matters in the content and context of the board meeting increase satisfaction of board members?

• Is it possible to include biblical and other text study in the actual decision making of a synagogue board?

• What should be the role of individual or group prayer (other than the customary opening and closing "bookend prayers") in the context of board meetings?

• In what way is concern for the religious life of the congregation demonstrated in the planning of the agenda and the conduct of board meetings?

• What do board members value, and how is this demonstrated in board actions and activities?

The following are examples of possible subject matter for board discussion.

• Introduction of a board agenda that groups topics according to Jewish concepts such as *tzedakah* and *mitzvot*.

• A ceremony that establishes the board's relationship to the Covenant (*brit*) and an explicit attempt to describe the board's work in relationship to various Covenant stories.

• Identification of leadership based on biblical, rabbinic, and later stories. We can still be guided, in speech and action, by the examples of Abraham, Sarah, Moses, Miriam, Ruth, Esther, Beruriah, Akiba, and the Baal Shem Tov, among many others.

• Consideration of when and how to implement new religious practices in the congregation. How do such practices come to be accepted? How do rituals grow and take on new meanings? A congregation and its leadership have the right and the responsibility to introduce new obligations (*mitzvot*) in response to changing historical conditions or to reinterpret old ones in new ways.

• Framing of a policy for supporting the synagogue, based on the laws of righteous giving or charity (*tzedakah*).

Take the agenda for your next board meeting — or the minutes of the last — and check all the items pertaining to worship, study of Torah, or religious commitment. How much time was allocated for these matters in comparison with all other matters? Were such matters left to the "professionals" to deal with outside the board meetings, or for discussion of a different nature in the synagogue's adult education courses? Remember, it is the task of trustees to govern so that the synagogue provides the Jewish content you want for yourself and for your family, neighbors, and friends.

Dr. Neil Gillman, professor of philosophy at the Jewish Theological Seminary of America, writes: "Every single decision that a congregation reaches in what transpires within the walls of a synagogue and within the parameters of congregational life must be seen as encouraging or discouraging specific models of Jewish expression. It pervades the budgetary process; it influences the work of a search committee that is seeking a rabbi or cantor for the congregation; it affects the decisions of the architect who is designing the sacred space in which worship takes place. It affects how the space within the synagogue building is apportioned. Educationally it influences the choice of a curriculum, of a textbook and of teachers to serve as models. It permeates the messages that are conveyed by the rabbi in teaching, preaching and counseling work. In short, it is simply omnipresent."[5]

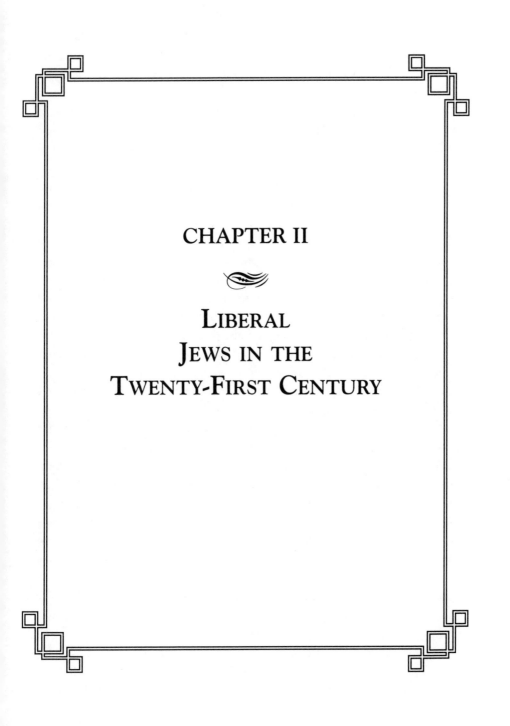

# CHAPTER II

# LIBERAL
# JEWS IN THE
# TWENTY-FIRST CENTURY

How each of us interprets being a liberal Jew in the twenty-first century may differ, but we can find in Reform Judaism a range of options for religious expression. Each of us makes decisions from among these options; that is the glory of belonging to a liberal movement. We must, however, work our way out of the unhappy situation where religious obligations for one class of persons, referred to as "professionals," are viewed as mandatory, while for other persons, referred to as "laity," religious obligations are often viewed as optional.

Rabbi Daniel Polish of Vassar Temple in Poughkeepsie, New York, suggests that each board ask itself the following questions: "Are we prepared to talk about religion that on some level makes demands that may look like deprivations? Are we prepared to be involved with the whole of one's life and not just some aspects? Are we prepared to encourage people to engage in practices that do set them apart from the mainstream of American life?" If we say "no" to any of these questions, he posits, we are not serious. "If we proceed," Rabbi Polish says, "we must acknowledge that what will flow from our work will entail radical changes in the ways that synagogues function; in the content and mode of our educational system; in the way we understand what it means to be a Reform Jew."[1]

The responsibility of synagogue volunteer leaders — indeed, of all Jews — is to become educated so as to make informed choices for ourselves, help others define their standard of commitment, and show respect for others' choices. A very real question is whether Reform Jews, nourished on freedom of choice, can be drawn to accept *any* authority. The founders of Reform Judaism emphasized that the Jew's ethical responsibilities, imposed by God, left each Jew free to choose behavior demonstrating his or her religious identity. Nevertheless, many Reform Jews today interpret individual choice to mean a legitimate freedom to choose little or no observance. Rabbi Dow Marmur of Holy Blossom Temple, Toronto, interprets this to mean that they joined the synagogue "to be identified, not to practice," and so "they see their non-practice as an authentic expression of Reform Judaism." He sees a "collusion of the synagogue" in accepting a financial commitment as the only commitment expected of its congregants.[2]

Rabbi Marmur does not postulate "perfect faith as a prerequisite for [board] service," but he observes that "it is difficult, if not impossible, to serve God in collective action without seeking God in personal reflection and study." He says, "Seeking the will of God is our most sacred task," and adds, "The task is so sacred that it makes the sacrifice of popularity insignificant in comparison to the opportunity to be a faithful servant of the God of Israel and the people of Israel. That's why, despite all the burdens, leadership in the Jewish community is a privilege."

Rabbi Peter Knobel of Beth Emet The Free Synagogue in Evanston, Illinois, develops a similar theme: "Synagogues are institutions in search of community. They are supermarkets of services that aspire to be temples for worship of the living God. They behave like secular corporations, but wish to be understood as sacred places. Style and substance are often confused. Key to transformation is a partnership between volunteer leadership and professional leadership. Key to transformation is a partnership among the lay leadership itself. The operative word of all these relationships must be *brit*, covenant. All must see themselves as God's stewards who faithfully tend an orchard entrusted to their care. The manual for nurturing healthy fruitful trees is the sacred text."[3]

If Jews take their Judaism seriously, they must take their volunteer positions of trust seriously. The converse is also true. If Jews take their volunteer roles seriously, they must take their Judaism seriously. The responsibilities of board members — like those of the rabbi and cantor — do not end in the sanctuary. They include defining how to help the trustees themselves, their families, and their fellow congregants to grow Jewishly, both within the synagogue and in their personal daily living.

What kind of synagogue can make this possible? It is one whose organization includes the following characteristics:

• It has a clear vision of why it exists and what it is trying to accomplish — a vision that is developed and shared by the volunteer leadership, rabbis and cantor, professional staff, and congregation — and it has a system for evaluating and adjusting that vision as necessary on a periodic basis.

• It is well managed, with appropriate planning, financial, and communications programs.

• It constantly questions how it can accomplish its mission more effectively and focuses on projects critical to its mission.

• It maintains a "big-picture focus" and strives to understand and participate in movement-wide activities of the Reform movement, such as supporting the State of Israel, assisting Jews in the former Soviet Union, and fostering the development of liberal Judaism in Israel and worldwide under the auspices of the World Union for Progressive Judaism/ARZA. At the same time, an effective board is intent on providing high-quality services to its own membership.

• It establishes a structure and operating philosophy that maximize opportunities for elected leadership and professional staff to combine their respective skills. Congregants play their role best when professionals assist them in defining the issues and counsel them in their decision making. Failure by professionals to respect the role of congregants, develop new leadership, and support appropriate congregational responsibility is a source of trouble.

• It provides fresh input and perspectives via changes in the volunteer leadership. Note that there are some people who can best serve the synagogue in capacities other than trustee, perhaps in ad hoc roles where their professional and technical skills are fully utilized over a short period of time in the solution of specific problems and after which they can feel a sense of satisfaction and be thanked for their contribution.

• It fosters a striving for quality and excellence in every facet of its work.

• It creates an atmosphere in which board members feel personally connected within the board, and in which each trustee feels connected to the members of the congregation. An atmosphere of trust and mutual respect is established, and trustees model hospitality.

• It takes a high ethical position in all of its dealings, including arrangements with people — staff professionals, volunteers, and synagogue members — and with firms doing business with the synagogue. Boards need to be alert to the entire range of possibilities for conflicts of interest. A policy defining conflict and identifying ways for dealing with it will save board members from embarrassment or malfeasance. A synagogue policy should include the following: a statement of the ethical principles that will guide the board's decision making; a reflection of local circumstances and mandates as well as community standards and expectations; a definition of the procedures individual board members and the board as a whole will take in the event that a conflict of interest occurs; and an annual, written statement from all trustees stating that they are unaware of any existing or potential conflicts or outlining any specific conflicts of which the board is aware.

• It is truly a community that cares about and for its members.

# CHAPTER III

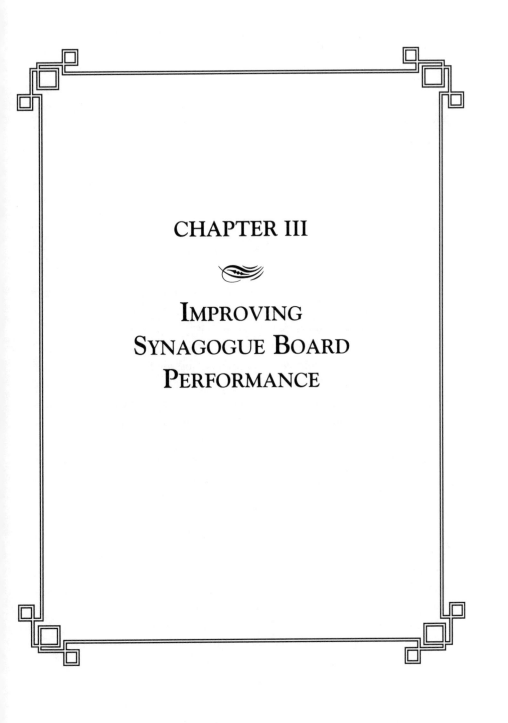

## IMPROVING
## SYNAGOGUE BOARD
## PERFORMANCE

Most synagogue board members accept their positions because they believe the synagogue needs them and that they have something to offer. Yet trustees who are competent people in other aspects of their lives — making sound decisions in their business or professional lives or on the boards of other organizations — frequently become immobilized in the synagogue. Although they view the synagogue as the primary vehicle by which a vision of Reform Judaism is communicated, many board members are frustrated and angered, or at best bored, by what could have been an ennobling leadership experience. They feel that they have not been effectively used and that their time has been wasted. They want a great deal of information, and in many cases it is not offered to them, or at least not in a form that is helpful in their policy-making roles. Some synagogues spend more time figuring out ways to make board members "feel" as if they are involved than in actually involving them.

"The key to making a board effective is not to talk about its function but to organize its work,"[1] says Dr. Peter Drucker, professor at Claremont Graduate School in California. He writes that nonprofit institutions used to say, "We don't pay volunteers so we cannot make demands upon them." Now they are more likely to say, "Volunteers must get far greater satisfaction from their accomplishments and make a greater contribution precisely because they do not get a paycheck." He observes that "The steady transformation of the volunteer from well-meaning amateur to professional, unpaid staff member is the most significant development in the nonprofit sector." Dr. Drucker concludes that if nonprofit organizations want to attract and hold knowledgeable workers in jobs in which they contribute to society as volunteers, "they have to put their competence and knowledge to work. They have to offer meaningful work."[2]

Improving the performance of synagogue boards begins with the identification of potential future leaders by the nominating committee. There is no more important group than that charged with ensuring continuity of leadership for the congregation. The committee may begin deliberations as much as six to twelve months in advance of making its recommendations of men and women for election as board members and as officers.

The trustee development process, begun by the nominating committee, leads through committees to the board itself in a program of shared responsibility — shared between the individual trustee and the synagogue — designed to enable individuals to become more knowledgeable and more productive in the positions to which they have been elected. Presumably, the trustees know that they have to invest time and energy to make their contribution. But do the requirements of board participation far exceed the expectations of the new trustees? Many a promising new board member has failed to live up to what the group expected of him or her because of a lack of adequate orientation. Too late do the new members discover what they have let themselves in for. Before accepting an invitation to participate, prospective board members should know as much as possible about the responsibilities they are to assume.

What should the individual trustee do to ensure his or her getting the best possible introduction to service as a board member? The following checklist offers some steps that should be suggested to new trustees to help them become oriented and informed about their new roles:

• Read the bylaws of the congregation, which describe the structure of the board and the functions of its standing committees.

• Acquire a board calendar and a schedule of meetings. Review the minutes of recent board meetings.

• Become acquainted with those aspects of the programmatic life of the synagogue (such as youth activities, festival observances, Sisterhood or Brotherhood programs, or the religious school) with which you may be less familiar.

• Become familiar with the synagogue's financial policies: with its budget, financial reports, and operating statements; with its administrative structure; and with the physical plant.

• Ask for a clear account of the division of responsibilities among the board, the rabbi, the cantor, and the professional staff, including the administrator, the education director, and any others.

• Learn what is expected of an individual trustee in regard to committee work, fund-raising, participation in worship, and other synagogue activities.

An effective board ensures that a meaningful trustee orientation process exists and that all members go through it. James Orlikoff, president of Orlikoff & Associates in Chicago, cites four purposes of trustee orientation: "to give the new trustee a general sense of the environment and context within which the institution must function; to outline the culture, values and norms of the organization, and show how the board acts to perpetuate these key organizational characteristics; to provide new trustees with a sense of the [institution's] history, so that they gain a complete understanding of the [institution] and are then able to contribute to its continuity; to explain the values of the board itself — that is, how the board's values and culture affect the process of governance."[3]

A good orientation program is the first step toward effective governance, but it is only the beginning of the trustee's education. Ongoing education is a cornerstone of board development and effective governance, especially in rapidly changing times. Many boards have found it helpful to appoint a committee on governing board development. Once such a committee is formed, the following can be some of its responsibilities:

• To assess the educational and informational needs of the board and to continue this assessment on at least an annual basis

• To make sure the annual operating budget contains adequate funds in a specific line item to cover proposed activities for board development

• To make sure that criteria for selection of new board members are developed

• To make sure that new board members are oriented to their responsibilities as trustees

• To ensure that educational programs and resources appropriate to the board's needs are planned and promoted.

• To evaluate on an annual basis the performance of each trustee, with respect to participation, attendance, and continuing education

• To establish liaisons with other synagogue governing boards in the same area for the purpose of collaborating on joint trustee educational efforts

Many synagogues conduct board retreats, seeing in them opportunities for trustees to focus on important issues, get to know each other better, and work on team-building skills. Retreats also offer orientation and education opportunities for new trustees.

Will trustees take time to participate in board retreats? Research indicates that they will do so, provided that the content is perceived to be relevant, the demands of the program are not excessive, the format is attractive, the trustees are involved from beginning to end in formulating the program, and the experience is positive and meaningful.

Leading or serving on board committees frequently offers trustees the opportunity to assist the congregation in a meaningful way. (See Appendix A for a sample list of synagogue committees.) How many committees should a synagogue have? There are several schools of thought. One view is that everyone on the board should lead his or her own committee. The other extreme wants to get rid of virtually all committees. An intermediate, and more sensible, approach is to keep all needed committees and to maintain flexibility in responding to new issues by creating ad hoc task forces rather than new standing committees. A task force can either resolve the issue or refine it to such an extent that it can be dealt with by a standing committee. It may also draw on special skills and interests of members of the congregation.

The result of reducing the number of committees to those you really need is a more efficient organization. But like any form of change, a streamlining of committees can meet with resistance from incumbent chairpersons who have held positions for many years. The fact that many younger board members are critical of board performance may reflect their feelings of under involvement in key positions. The combining of committees may allow a congregation to rethink the issues of committee chairs and committee makeup, creating an opportunity for different — and sometimes younger — people to become involved in significant posts.

Discussions with board members and rabbis indicate that both groups are frequently dissatisfied with the length of board meetings and with what is accomplished, believing also that the meetings do not reflect Jewish values in either substance or tone. They are too long, and time is eaten up by oral reports that could better have been presented as concisely written reports distributed in advance by mail or e-mail. Another improvement may be setting firm times for beginning and ending a meeting and sticking with them. Agenda items should be prioritized, with time restrictions identified.

Rabbis and synagogue administrators must encourage the best use of trustees' enthusiasm and convey to governing board members the importance of their contributions. A rabbi or staff member who complains about poor attendance, low interest, and lack of available time on the part of trustees should examine his or her expectations of the board. Synagogue staff must encourage trustees' initiative in planning, policy making, and governing board development. To do so, staff must accept the governing board as a vital part of the organization. A board that challenges, questions, or rejects recommendations is providing input from its perspective. An effective board, in other words, insists on being effective.

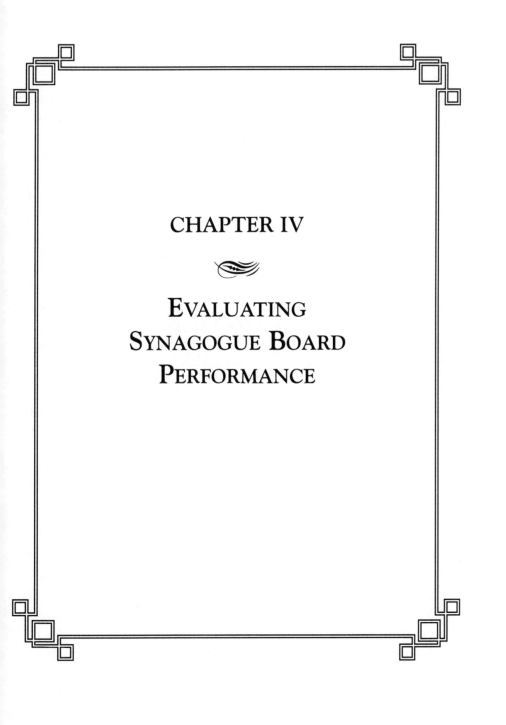

# CHAPTER IV

# EVALUATING SYNAGOGUE BOARD PERFORMANCE

The willingness of a synagogue board to evaluate its own effectiveness is a positive sign. Serious trustees want to be challenged, and they recognize their potential even if at times they doubt that the synagogue recognizes it. Such trustees ask themselves whether they are doing a good job, but most synagogues are not prepared to help them deal with that question. Most boards review performance only after something has gone awry; however, the board that does not regularly review its performance invites trouble. Self-evaluation allows a board to identify its strengths as well as those areas where changes and improvements are necessary.

It has been suggested that reviewing board performance may be the last of the unmet needs in organizational life. Why? First, standards of performance have not emerged for boards. Second, the willingness of a board to critically and objectively evaluate its own effectiveness is a sign of vitality, but not many boards show such vitality. Third, some boards have considered undertaking such assessment but have demurred because they felt unsure how to proceed. Fourth, individuals hesitate to (openly) evaluate fellow volunteers because trusteeship is viewed as a gift of a person's time and talent, and it seems inappropriate to measure the value of a gift. Many board members are also uncomfortable with the knowledge that they themselves will be evaluated.

There are compelling reasons for synagogues to develop performance standards for their governing body and for individual trustees. Self-assessment makes the board more aware of its potential in governance and of barriers to effective performance. An evaluation may reveal opportunities for improvement, such as establishing new criteria in selecting and retaining board members or paying greater attention to building a congregational community.

If a synagogue board evaluation process exists, all board members should be aware of it and should view it positively as a program to achieve and maintain quality standards. Furthermore, all board members should participate in the evaluation process, and a sufficiently positive attitude should be developed so as to ensure full support for implementation and action as a result of the evaluation.

Trustee performance evaluation can be done by some outside group, such as management or governance consultants, or it can be done from within. Outside groups, while providing objectivity, may lack familiarity with the synagogue and its problems; their analysis and conclusions may be superficial, not to mention expensive. Internal review generally seems the most practical road to follow. But who should do the evaluation? Since this kind of evaluation will be new to virtually all synagogues, a suitable locus must be found. Because the nominating committee is charged with recommending trustees, as well as the slate of officers, the nominating committee may be the most appropriate group for undertaking this task as an extension of its responsibility. (One other group for consideration is the trustee development committee now being appointed in some synagogues.) Measurement of competency, of course, begins with the nominating committee's selection process, and the committee thereby bears some of the burden for its nominees' performance record.

Evaluation is a two-step process. The first step is to obtain and assess information on performance. The second is to place that performance against some standard. The purpose of the evaluation is to build on strengths and to overcome weaknesses.

Measurement of board performance includes answering such questions as the following: Does the board carry out its responsibilities in the organizational framework outlined in its own bylaws? Do all trustees exercise their responsibility for providing input into the decision-making process? Do minutes indicate the adoption of timely courses of action? Does the board act appropriately on reports it receives?

Since all governing board performance is the collective result of the individual activities of each of its members, an evaluation review of each member would seem in keeping with sound organizational practice. At the board level the structure provides for group action, minimizing the impact of individual performance. Nevertheless, collective evaluation without discrimination between individual performances denies that such important differences clearly exist.

In setting its own standards, the evaluating group must define the characteristics of a good trustee. Here are a few to examine: has skills or experiences not duplicated on the board; engages in independent self-education to help meet responsibilities; understands the synagogue's philosophy and plans, and relevant matters on the local, national, or even international level; prepares carefully for board meetings; shows an interest in long-range planning; has future leadership potential; serves on committees and executes committee responsibilities; regularly attends board meetings; and is personally committed to Judaism, demonstrating this by living Jewishly, with attention to performance of *mitzvot* and dedication to the work of the synagogue.

When a congregation finds such a role model, it must take care not to work him or her to the point of burnout. There's a saying that twenty percent of board members are overextended and do eighty percent of the work. They are burning out and leaving before their time. Discussion about burnout always draws sympathetic reaction from volunteer leaders. Trustee burnout is usually marked by changes in a trustee's behavior and attitude, negatively affecting the level and quality of the trustee's involvement. For example, the trustee may stop attending most board or committee meetings, stop reading board agenda materials; demonstrate interest in only one issue; resist change or new ideas; or begin questioning his or her own board membership.

Here are suggestions for preventing trustee burnout: ensure that board work is evenly distributed among all trustees; establish time limits for board meetings, and stick to them; and limit trustees' terms of office so as to encourage diversity of membership and fresh thinking.

Any discussion of board evaluation must not overlook the special position of the president, who serves as the board's chair. Not only must he or she exhibit the skills required of and perform the tasks listed for individual members, but, in addition, the chairperson must be evaluated in terms of his or her ability to help the board accomplish its goals. Does the chair guide the board toward meeting new challenges? Is the chair a good communicator with other board members, the clergy, and the staff? Does the chair counsel other board members and assess their performance? Does the chair facilitate relations between the synagogue, including its board members, and other synagogues, institutions, and agencies? (See Appendix C, "What a New Synagogue President Needs to Know," and Appendix D, "Questions a Synagogue President Should Ask After One Year in Office.")

All of the above suggest that no matter with what trepidation a board considers the matter of self-evaluation, it is one of the necessities of organizational life.

# CHAPTER V

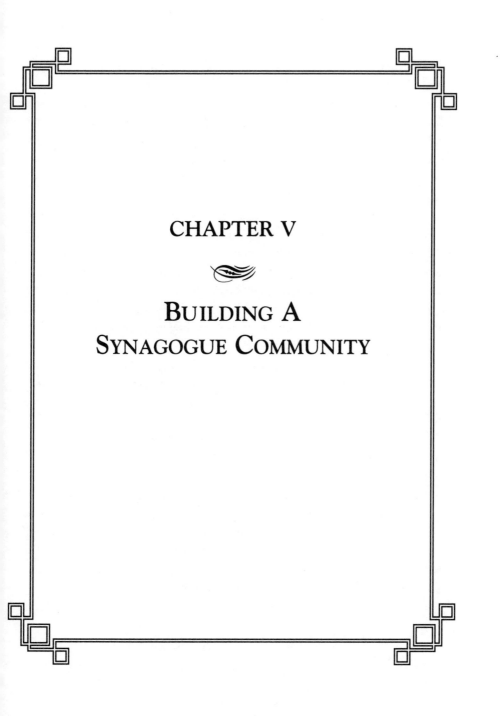

# BUILDING A
# SYNAGOGUE COMMUNITY

Research indicates that many people join a congregation because they want to be part of a community, and not necessarily because they are committed to a particular set of religious doctrines. This is noted by the sociologist Egon Mayer, who observes that "for an awful lot of people today, the particular brand name of the congregation is less important than the people, the friends, the fellowship, even child care."[1] While we frequently identify our religious affiliation by declaring that our synagogue is Reform, Ward Clark Roof, another student of American religion, cautions that "a denomination as a locus of identity doesn't carry much strength. What they're looking for is a spiritual home that feels comfortable and appealing."[2]

A major challenge to synagogue boards is to foster the development of a sense of "community." For this discussion, "community" is defined as "a group of people who are similarly motivated to achieve a common goal and who are organized and willing to assume common obligations toward that end." A key question for synagogue boards to answer is: What policies and program priorities will assure congregations that every facet of a synagogue, including the physical facility itself, is inclusive and serves all members of the community?

If community feeling is to coalesce in the synagogue, it will be the result of detailed, painstaking hard work. There are predictably times when each of us needs to be part of a community — when, as Rabbi Marmur says, we find our "wholeness or our potential only as members of a larger group." He emphasizes that "communities are not created by board or clergy, but only by all of their members; and those who stand outside of a community feel excluded, however great their need. People who have not joined in building a community don't have a full sense of it when they need it."

The Reform movement and each of our synagogues must work to strengthen the ties that connect us to each other. We must build synagogue communities in which people have choices, and communities that will be able to accommodate divergent subcommunities while maintaining common bonds. One of the major challenges facing congregations experiencing growth will be to address the meaning of community and how to attain and maintain it.

It is the board's responsibility to understand and develop the Reform ideal of the synagogue as a caring community. That entails moving congregations toward a useful role in meeting more of the pressing needs of families, youth, seniors, single men and women, Jews-by-Choice, gays and lesbians, and the intermarried. There must be an attempt to respond to human needs, whether through the efforts of volunteers and staff at the synagogue or through activities carried out jointly by the synagogue and other agencies. Neither synagogues nor federations nor Jewish social service agencies, acting alone, can sufficiently address the range of problems and reach the numbers of those Jewish people who need the services of a caring community. Together they can maximize human services of high quality for more people. Such joint efforts put Jewish precepts into practice and add a significant dimension to the work of the synagogue board of trustees.

Dr. David Teutsch, president of the Reconstructionist Rabbinical College, reminds us that "Jewish religious life requires involvement in Jewish community — Jewish community not in the abstract collective but in the particularity of a local community rich in custom, interpersonal contact and local distinctiveness. It is in the context of community that our search for transcendent connection and meaningful daily living takes place. When Jews have no roots in such a vital community, Jewish religion loses its context and therefore its clarity and focus. 'Life is with people' is not just a slogan; it is a theological assertion."[3]

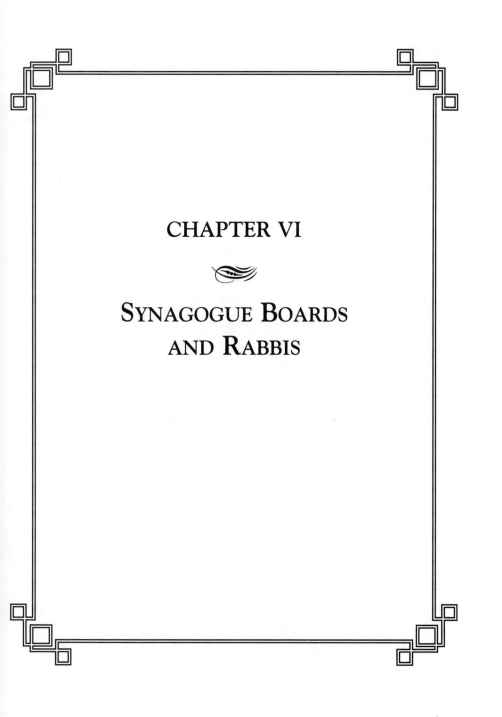

# CHAPTER VI

# SYNAGOGUE BOARDS
# AND RABBIS

Synagogue boards and rabbis inevitably see the world from different perspectives. These differences can give rise to different approaches on issues, and even to conflict. To minimize areas of potential conflict, here are some questions for consideration:

• Does the board meet with the rabbi to help him or her develop annual goals and objectives?

• Does the board effectively monitor and evaluate institutional performance, including the impact of worship services?

• Does the rabbi have an opportunity to participate in significant decision making and to provide feedback to the board on the implementation of board decisions and on their implications for future planning?

• Does the board work closely with the rabbi in developing long-range goals and policies and in regularly evaluating the synagogue's plans and programs to ensure that long-range plans are carried out?

Each congregation needs to study its own governing structure and evolve the most satisfying and productive relationship between the rabbi and the board. Rabbis and volunteer leadership need to join together to achieve mutual expectations and aspirations for their congregation. (In this connection, special attention is called to the useful booklet, *Guidelines for Rabbinical-Congregational Relationships*, adopted by the Union of American Hebrew Congregations and the Central Conference of American Rabbis in 1984 and reprinted in 1990.) Achieving this collaboration is sometimes difficult because many rabbis and volunteer leaders have not been trained to think in terms of shared leadership and are unsure how to achieve it. Furthermore, even as we say that we should sensitively address the delicate interface between rabbi and board, and work to develop trust between them, recent years have seen growing problems in some congregations. The shared dissatisfaction of some rabbis and board members with their relationship provides an excellent opportunity for a redefinition of synagogue leadership as partnership (*brit*) and sacred duty (*mitzvah*), and offers a chance for rabbis, cantors, education directors, administrators, and trustees to view themselves as *klei kodesh*, people with the common objective of helping congregations to discover the holy.

Board members need to understand that the committee variously known as worship, ritual, or religious practices generates more controversy and concern for some rabbis than almost any other part of synagogue organizational life. This occurs because the appointment of the committee or task force is not preceded by frank discussion between the rabbi and the congregation's volunteer leadership. For many congregations the worship committee evolved as a sounding board invited by the rabbi, but in recent years it has taken on new roles. Is it a decision-making body? What do both parties really want to achieve through this medium? What is considered negotiable and what is not? What is the role of the board vis-à-vis the worship committee?

Many worship committees have been identified with important "housekeeping" activities — for example, scheduling ushers, determining the number or placement of extra chairs needed for the High Holy Days, or overseeing the parking lot to facilitate entry and exit when double services are necessary. These tasks must be undertaken, if necessary by the worship committee; but all too frequently they become the committee's sole tasks or major tasks, denying a sense of challenge or involvement with the worship itself.

Synagogue boards need to explore with the rabbi and cantor how to raise the sights of worship committees, without their neglecting the housekeeping tasks that they have been asked to oversee and that are critical to the overall functioning of the synagogue. Many worship committees devote significant time to organizational issues surrounding holidays and special events without considering the theological underpinning of these events. It is necessary to address the "why" behind the observance and its rituals and to link it to the theological frame in which the service and associated events are viewed. This is particularly true when the area being addressed is how the congregation celebrates and observes Shabbat, which most congregants do not observe in a traditionally discernible way. How to bring about significant Shabbat observance by synagogue members can be a real challenge to rabbis, cantors, and worship committees.

The eventual success or failure of Reform Judaism begins with its ability to create a community so informed as to be able to make choices and commitments. To create an informed community may require a number of carefully timed steps of teaching and discussion, originating with the board and developed more deeply by the worship committee. If the board is to be supportive of the worship committee, then board members need to acquire background on how the Reform movement has understood itself on basic religious questions.

Rabbi David Lieb of Temple Beth El in San Pedro, California, has examined the role of the worship committee as an agent of change. Commenting on his survey of fifty congregations throughout the United States, Rabbi Lieb wrote: "In sum, its conclusions point the way for the work of worship committees that encourage lay empowerment and participation rather than simply rubber-stamping the ideas of the rabbi. It may well take a fine balancing act to maintain the rabbi's traditional authority, but it seems to me

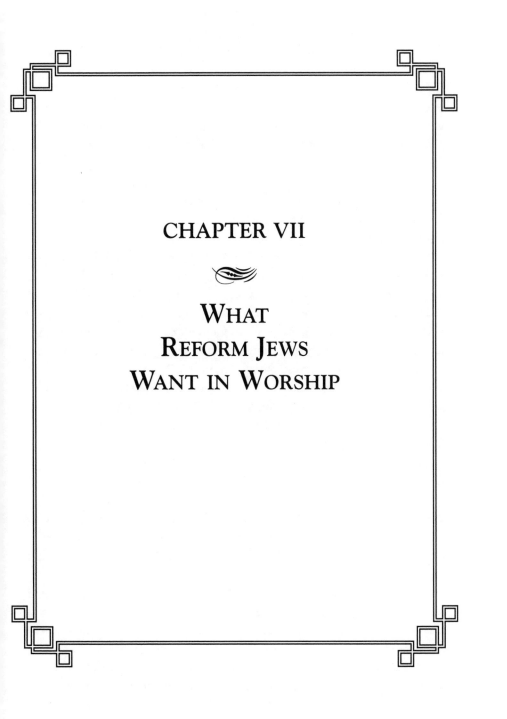

# CHAPTER VII

## WHAT REFORM JEWS WANT IN WORSHIP

Because the synagogue is above all a religious community, the assessment of the congregation's worship experience must be a priority for the synagogue's board, as it is for the rabbis and cantor. This is not meant as a challenge to the traditional role of the clergy, but as an acknowledgment that all will benefit from a mutual sharing of responsibility. Even if the board chooses to identify a group of knowledgeable and committed synagogue members to give attention to worship, the board never relinquishes its accountability for oversight.

How do Reform Jews assess their congregational worship experience? What changes would they advocate to enhance congregational worship? Can they really express themselves on these questions? The answer to the last question is that they can and do.

Research as to how congregations — their rabbis and membership — can participate together in a congregational self-assessment of their major regular worship service was part of a recent Central Conference of American Rabbis project. Forty-seven Reform congregations in North America organized worship self-study teams of ten to fourteen people whose range in age, frequency of attendance, and liturgical skills were typical of the congregation as a whole. The teams studied their Friday night Shabbat services. This study resulted in a "snapshot" of what Reform congregants look for in their worship. The methodology, which was found useful by the participating congregations, is offered for further use in Appendix E, "Procedure for Self-Study of Congregational Worship."

Congregants participating in this self-assessment project wanted, through Shabbat worship, to link themselves to the Jewish people and to affirm as a community the meaning of the Jewish experience as enshrined in Torah and prayerbook and interpreted by Reform Judaism. They wanted to be part of a worshiping community that affirms and celebrates Jewish ethical precepts and studies them as a guide to daily living for individuals and for the group.

Congregants said they come to the synagogue from the outside world in search of an extraordinary experience. They described successful worship as the experience of the transcendent, with prayer as one of the tools of worship. Experiencing a sense of peace, of respite, and of community were commonly used phrases to describe a successful service. Almost every congregant spoke of the power of music in worship. Congregants believe that worship is an art which can be taught and learned, and that it should take place in a community which is egalitarian and participatory. They acknowledged the difficulty of satisfying an increasingly diverse community but expressed a genuine desire that a service say nothing to inhibit full participation and full identification with the liturgical vision. Other important issues included accessibility, signing for the hearing impaired, large-print prayerbooks, the presence of greeters, and the friendliness of congregants at the Oneg Shabbat.

While technology has made it possible for each congregation to become a prayerbook publisher, interviewed congregants almost uniformly said that they want a common prayerbook so that regardless of what Reform synagogue they find themselves in, they will know the liturgy being prayed. They feel that using a common prayerbook helps them to become part of a larger Reform community with continuity to the Reform past as well as to the longer history of Judaism.

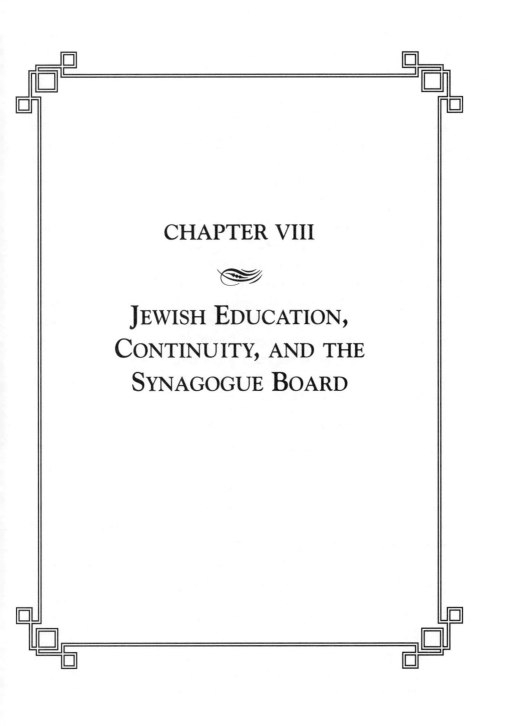

CHAPTER VIII

JEWISH EDUCATION,
CONTINUITY, AND THE
SYNAGOGUE BOARD

In *Pirke Avot* (2:8), our tradition teaches us that the more Torah, the more life. Reaffirming this wisdom in recent years, many leaders, commissions, and studies have concluded that Jewish education is the key to the continuity of a vibrant and committed Jewish people. In an age where much about life, from child rearing to spirituality, is learned through books, courses, speakers, the Internet, and peers rather than in one's childhood home, Jewish education plays a significant role in passing the Torah, and its values and ideals, from generation to generation. Education creates community by contributing to an individual's sense of a shared vision, purpose, history, and culture with other Jews.

The changing panorama of Jewish education presents many challenges to congregations and their boards. The key questions that each board needs to answer are: (1) What is the place of learning in our congregation? (2) Who are the learners? (3) What is the relationship between the congregation and the panoply of Jewish communal institutions that are working together for the continuity and strengthening of Jewish life? (4) In what ways does the congregation support Jewish educators, both teachers and administrators? (5) What are the roles of the board and the education committees with respect to Jewish learning in our congregation? These questions will be discussed below.

### 1. What is the place of learning in our congregation?

The focus of learning varies among congregations. In some congregations, formal learning programs are the means for transmitting Jewish knowledge, skills, and values to a specified population of children, families, or adults. In other congregations, learning socializes members into the practices, norms, and values of the congregation. Learning in still other congregations is used as a vehicle for addressing particular life-cycle or age challenges such as birth, marriage, death, coping with an illness, bar or bat mitzvah, or choosing Judaism. For others, learning is an integral part of congregational life, informing action in the realms of worship, social action, and ritual and holiday observance as well as influencing family life and congregational decision making and priority setting.

In any congregation, worship and learning need to be inextricably tied together: learning enriches the worship experience and heightens the sense of spirituality; learning helps increase the significance of prayer. A deeper understanding of the prayers, practices, and Jewish conceptions of God contributes to connecting these critical parts of the worship experience to one's life.

---

This chapter was written by Roberta Louis Goodman, R.J.E., Ed.D. She is a past president of the National Association of Temple Educators.

Congregations make statements about the value of Jewish learning and the honor (*kavod*) due to the learned in many ways. For example, does the board engage in the study of Jewish texts? How is the role of the education director valued? In what ways are adult learners publicly recognized? Both actual and symbolic statements are critical to reinforcing the value of learning within the congregation.

### 2. Who are the learners?

Clarifying the place of learning in the congregation should help answer this question. Jewish tradition upholds the importance of lifelong learning. Continuous, formalized educational institutions were the province of both adults and children throughout our history. Yet the 1990 Jewish population study suggested that although the overwhelming majority of Jewish children receive some formal Jewish education, less than 20 percent of adults participate in Jewish learning opportunities.

More and more congregations are developing educational programs to address the learning needs of adults and families as well as children. In addition to the usual Hebrew and religious schools, many congregations have preschools, some have day schools, a few have Jewish camps, others have summer programs, and most have informal educational programs like retreats or youth groups. Most congregations have some sort of family education programming. It is predicted that the next major spurt in demand for Jewish learning will arise among the growing population of older adults, particularly well-educated baby boomers. This aging population is likely to seek learning of all types to enrich their lives as empty nesters and retirees.

### 3. What is the relationship between the congregation and the panoply of Jewish communal institutions that are working together for the continuity and strengthening of Jewish life?

Not only do congregations have a multitude of Jewish educational programs, but so do local organizations like community and Reform day schools, preschools, Jewish community centers, Hadassah, federations, and central agencies for Jewish education. Regional and national groups, including the UAHC, sponsor educational offerings such as *kallot*, Elderhostel programs, camps, youth groups, and much more.

The results from the 1990 Jewish population study suggest that the more Jewish educational experiences in the variety of venues — religious school, summer camp, Israel experience, etc.— the more likely the individual will be committed to living as a Jew in adulthood. The challenge for congregations and their boards is to encourage and even help make it possible for the learner to gain access to the wide range of Jewish educational experiences.

Congregations and federations in many communities are involved in Jewish educational planning efforts to improve Jewish education. Federations and foundations increasingly are providing funding — or at least seed money — for innovative Jewish educational programs and projects. Boards need to consider the ways these granting opportunities can be helpful. Reform congregations would do well to build relationships and develop programs and projects around common interests with other congregations and Jewish communal institutions to foster these opportunities.

*4. In what ways does the congregation support Jewish educators, both teachers and administrators?*

Critical to a successful educational program is a partnership between lay leaders and the education director. Board members should cultivate an institutional culture of respect and trust for their professionals in which growth is valued. At the same time, board and committee members should be knowledgeable about the educational program and about trends in Jewish education and the Reform movement.

Judaism views teaching as a sacred task. Qualified and committed personnel is the key ingredient to a good school. Leadership by an education director and a committed faculty makes a significant difference in the quality and delivery of Jewish education. The budget of most schools, if not congregations, is appropriately and heavily oriented to spending on personnel.

Over the last few decades, congregations have made great strides in increasing the status and role of the congregational educator. Many education directors have responsibility for educating families and adults, in addition to schooling children. Education directors should be viewed as part of the professional leadership team involved in envisioning, planning, and implementing the congregational program.

Board members need to consider a number of issues related to integrating the education director and teaching staff into the life of the congregation, promoting their professional growth, and recognizing their contribution to the congregation.

*5. What are the roles of the board and education committees, with respect to Jewish learning in our congregation?*

Paralleling the growth of educational programs for children, families, and adults is the emergence of numerous education committees. Most congregations have multiple education committees rather than a single committee. It is important that at least the chairs of these committees come together to share approaches, calendars, and resources.

Education committees, regardless of the population that they address, need to concern themselves with policy issues, budgeting, and programmatic needs. In the case of the religious school committee, some congregations separate the policy issues and budgeting from the programmatic needs by having a committee that handles the first two items and an organization of parents that handles the last. Education committees can be helpful to the professionals in forming and affirming the educational program's overall vision, direction, goals, and curriculum.

The relationship between the board and its education committees — their respective functions and roles — should be outlined from the beginning. Expectations should be shared with all involved. While a board is well advised to let its education committees do much of the work, the board needs information about committee work to fulfill its oversight function and inform decisions regarding priority setting and budgeting. In turn, education committees need to understand board priorities.

Answering the key questions presented here will help the board ensure a quality Jewish educational program for the congregation.

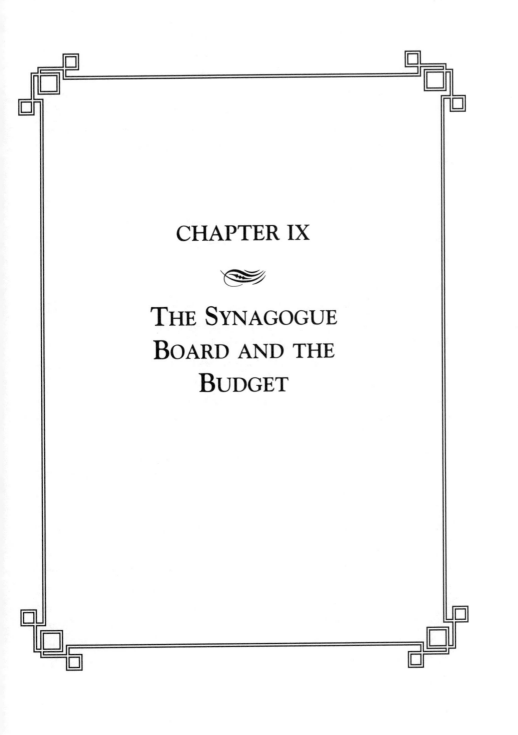

# CHAPTER IX

## THE SYNAGOGUE BOARD AND THE BUDGET

All synagogue trustees share a common responsibility: to build a vision and to assemble the means to carry it out. All board members must join in planning a sound financial future for the congregation.

Most programs with which the board deals have financial implications. Boards assess congregational priorities and programs to develop a financial strategy that includes both operating and capital budgets as defined below. As a practical matter, the board usually designates the finance committee or the executive committee to be responsible for careful monitoring of programs and their budgets; but the board itself should play the key role in the establishment of the priorities. Board members should receive financial reports on at least a quarterly basis. It is important that all congregational leaders maintain a realistic understanding of the synagogue's financial health.

Operating Budget

An operating budget is a projection of a synagogue's financial plans for the year ahead. (The fiscal year-end for synagogues, along with the Union of American Hebrew Congregations and the Hebrew Union College - Jewish Institute of Religion, is June 30, to conform with rabbinic and cantorial contracts.) The budget is developed collaboratively by volunteer and professional leadership. The budgeting process requires a climate of mutual trust and cooperation, encouraging freedom of expression and total honesty by all parties involved.

The budgeting process begins with the staff and operating committees closest to the program areas. There is a natural tendency at this stage to think in terms of "what we spent last year." Each operating committee is asked to review the current budget and its programming needs, and then to submit its request to the budget committee. Upon completion of the work of all the operating committees, the budget committee then needs to evaluate and integrate all the proposals into a draft of the proposed synagogue operating budget. To accomplish this, the budget committee needs to examine the expenses and to coordinate them with the revenues anticipated. At this stage the budget committee may have to look for modifications in programs or expenses to bring the budget into balance. When this has been completed, the budget committee forwards the budget for review and approval, first by the executive committee and then by the board.

The *Temple Management Manual*, published by the Union of American Hebrew Congregations and the National Association of Temple Administrators, says that a congregational budget is customarily broken down into the following categories:

1. Worship, including rabbinic and cantorial salary expenses, housing

arrangements, pension, life insurance, and other direct and indirect costs.

2. Education, including staff salaries and benefits, and all normal costs associated with the operation of a religious school and Hebrew school.

3. Membership Services and General Administration, sometimes referred to in smaller congregations as Office Operations.

4. Building Maintenance, providing the physical facilities for all congregational activities, and sometimes known as Buildings and Grounds.

5. Capital repairs and replacements, with an annual maintenance budget. Unless capital funds are available and have been earmarked for meeting the costs of repairs or replacements, it is essential that annual reserves be set aside for such expenses.

6. Special Programs, which may include a nursery school, day care center, or day camp serving a limited constituency among the membership. The basic question, to be answered by the board, is which of these activities are integral to the congregation's service program and which are ancillary. Such deliberations help clarify the costs to be assumed by the congregation, from those that need to be shared with members or non-members.

7. UAHC dues. It is imperative for congregations to build into their operating budgets their dues to support membership in the Union of American Hebrew Congregations. The UAHC offers programmatic and consultative services to congregations in North America and, working through the World Union for Progressive Judaism/ARZA, represents Reform Judaism around the world. Half of the congregational dues paid to the UAHC are allocated to the Hebrew Union College - Jewish Institute of Religion, which prepares rabbis, cantors, educators, and others for service within Reform synagogues.

Membership Dues

Generally speaking, congregations look to their membership dues for approximately 80 percent or more of their operating budget. While most congregations structure their dues on pro-rata formulas, with reductions for younger members and sometimes considerations for retired and widowed members as well, still other congregations have implemented dues based on "fair share" plans or suggested dues determined by various personal income levels. All congregations want to be known as warm and caring places where no individual or family is denied membership. At the present time it is estimated that 20 to 35 percent of synagogue members pay less than full dues, and congregations need to obtain funds to offset these lost revenues by establishing fees for some synagogue activities, encouraging voluntary contributions, organizing fund-raising activities, and charging rental fees for the use of synagogue property.

The *Temple Management Manual* observes that a majority of the respondents to a survey stated that they do not have any synagogue policy guidelines regarding dues payment in hardship cases. Congregational practices also vary widely regarding administrative procedures for making adjustments in dues. A special committee, composed of individuals recognized for maintaining confidentiality, and showing discretion and sensitivity, has been established in some congregations to work with the synagogue administrator in reviewing hardship cases.

### Charges and Fees

Many congregations charge fees for specific activities or events. The most common are those in connection with the religious school. The *Temple Management Manual* notes that there is general acceptance of school charges ranging from a small book fee to several hundred dollars. In some congregations, school costs are included in general membership dues; in others there is a user fee. Other legitimate charges relate to benefits received by individuals, such as participation in a congregational seder.

### Fund-raising

Because dues payments may not cover all programs and services, it is necessary to develop a disciplined approach to the identification, cultivation, and solicitation of gifts to make such programs and services available. Beginning in their orientation, board members should be educated about the synagogue's need for gifts and the role of individual trustees in acquiring gifts. Nevertheless, an ongoing effort is required to help board members learn how to be comfortable in that role. Service on the board makes clear that there are always needs for ongoing or special fund-raising efforts, ranging from annual free-will contributions to major capital-fund campaigns.

Additional sources of income for the congregational operating budget are a multitude of fund-raising events such as dinners, bazaars, art fairs, auctions, concerts, trips, speakers' forums, and so on. Specific congregational projects or programs may best be supported by donations to special-purpose funds. Other fees may be charged to individuals or to outside organizations that use the facilities for social or cultural events.

In all of its fund-raising activities, the synagogue counts on individual trustees to make "leadership" gifts commensurate with their resources. One hundred percent participation by trustees is symbolic of the board's commitment to the synagogue. Less than 100 percent participation by board members sets a poor example for others. If the board is not persuaded to meet the goal it sets for itself, it is unlikely that sufficient funds from other congregational members will be attracted. On the other hand, it is important to note that no one should be disqualified from board membership because of limited financial resources.

Capital Budget

The purpose of a capital budget is to provide for the maintenance and refurbishing of facilities that generally have a life of five to ten years, such as paint, decorating, replacement of carpeting, and heating and air conditioning systems, but not for any major expansion of facilities that may require a capital fund-raising campaign. A capital budget, like the operating budget, should be approved by the board of trustees. While it should be prepared annually, it should cover a three-to-five-year period. The capital budget should be funded through sources of funds such as a reserve built up by annual allocations from the operating budget or transfers from any other available restricted funds, gifts, and proceeds from the sale of any property. In contrast, capital expenditures funded by a special fund-raising campaign would include acquisition of property, construction of new facilities, the replacement of major equipment, and significant improvements including the reduction of deferred maintenance. The capital budget should emerge, in part, from collaborative long-range strategic planning by the board and its committees, because it may reflect decisions regarding capital fund-raising and the acquisition or disposition of property.

Endowment Fund

The purpose of the endowment fund is to provide for the funding of the future needs of the congregation — for example, expanded programming, improved Jewish education, and capital improvements and replacements, while lessening the need for special assessments and the burden of future dues increases. With the growing popularity of endowment funds in the institutional world, congregations — even smaller ones — should actively pursue the development of an endowment fund. Congregations should also encourage unrestricted gifts; those that are restricted must be approved by the board of trustees as consonant with the objectives and needs of the congregation. The investment and allocation of endowment funds should be supervised by a separately organized endowment investment committee appointed by the synagogue board, typically for staggered terms. This committee must be autonomous. The synagogue board should have no jurisdiction or control of the committee, except through the retirement and replacement of its members in accordance with synagogue bylaws.

Anthony Ruger, an expert in the financing of theological seminaries, suggests that the following practices for handling various funds should be stated explicitly by boards and be observed by both trustees and staff: "Endowment funds shall be held inviolate. Restricted funds shall be used only for the purpose specified by the donor. Designated funds shall be used only for the purpose designated by the board of trustees. Interfund borrowing is not allowed without prior approval of the board of trustees or the trustee committee to which the board has delegated authority. The transfer of funds from one to another shall require the approval of the board of trustees or the trustee committee to which the board has delegated authority."[1] He concludes that without such basic policies and practices, trustees risk legal liability, and donors and others may lose confidence in the leadership. Synagogues need to educate board members carefully on this issue.

Annual Audit

An annual audit of the congregation's financial statements should be conducted by independent certified public accountants (auditors) at the end of each fiscal year. The board is responsible for naming an audit committee and approving selection of the auditors. The functions of the audit committee are to recommend to the board the selection of the auditors, the scope of the audit, and the fees to be paid. The audit committee works with the auditors on the definition of their assignment and discusses with them their findings and recommendations. In addition to reviewing particular transactions and the construction of financial statements to assure their reliability to donors and trustees, the outside auditors examine the synagogue's methods or systems of accounting and control. At the conclusion of the auditors' work, and its review by the audit committee, the auditors prepare a "management letter" describing any problems identified, along with recommended solutions. These issues typically deal with internal controls and improving the efficiency of procedures. The chair of the audit committee should report to the board (or the finance or executive committee, as appropriate) on its meeting with the auditors and present any items in the audit report requiring board action. A copy of the audited financial statements should be made available to trustees.

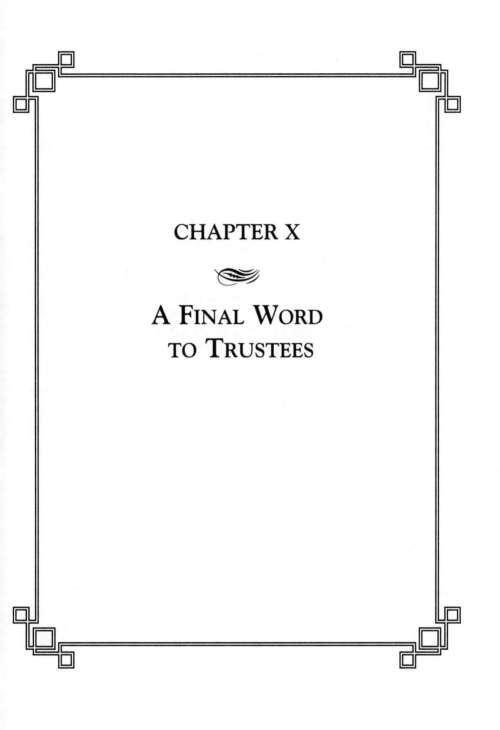

# CHAPTER X

# A FINAL WORD TO TRUSTEES

True leaders are people of substance, authenticity, and vision. They are seen to work hard to reach their goals. They show a commitment to their own personal development, and their ideas are fresh and innovative. Such synagogue leaders — clergy, other professionals, and volunteers —function on at least two levels: as individuals who are deeply committed Jews; and as individuals who are sensitive to the concerns of others, and who try to deal with those concerns in synagogues and other institutions and agencies through which Judaism is translated into the service of human need.

"No one can give our leaders a rule by which to distinguish an unworthy compromise or an overly idealistic demand for what, as best we can figure out, God wants of us in our particular here-and-now," says Dr. Eugene Borowitz, professor at Hebrew Union College-Jewish Institute of Religion. "That is where their leadership as well as their character and faith will be tested. . . . God calls us all to be holy not in some general, spiritual way but in the humdrum of making money and spending it, of working with some people and against the designs of others, of loving and hating and being indifferent, of the situations we are stuck with and those we can create to our will. Our Judaism seeks to make us realists who are not cynical, idealists who are not fools."[1]

Rabbi Marmur makes a final request to trustees: "Use your influence over our lives with utmost responsibility and great humility."

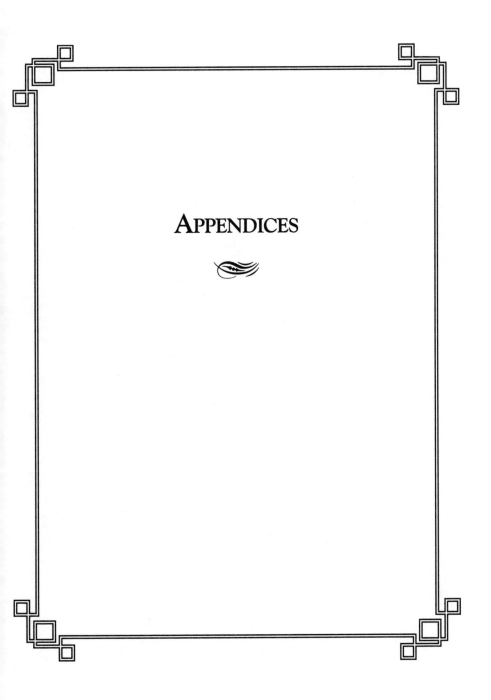

# APPENDICES

# Appendix A

## Sample List of Congregational Committees

Following is a list of committees, including a brief explanation of the typical responsibilities of each, frequently found in congregations. Committees may be logically grouped or combined to keep their number manageable. A congregation's committees may change as the needs and priorities of the congregation change. Note also that the *name* of a committee may change from congregation to congregation.

*Adult Education*: develops programs and designs curriculum for adult learning

*Budget*: projects annual income and expenses and makes periodic reports of income and expenditures to the board; coordinates preparation of the budget for board review

*Buildings and Grounds*: supervises buildings, grounds, equipment maintenance, and improvements; supervises the use of facilities

*Executive*: acts as an agent for the board, if so authorized, in time of emergency or between regularly scheduled meetings of the board

*Finance*: reviews the financial needs of the congregation; recommends investments; reviews financial reports to the board and congregation

*Interfaith Relations*: provides opportunities for programming and dialogue with non-Jewish groups in the community

*Leadership Development*: plans ways of identifying, training, and motivating leadership

*Library*: develops and plans utilization of the synagogue library

*Membership*: promotes and conserves congregational membership, and monitors the membership situation

*Music*: oversees the musical content of the synagogue program and arranges special musical programs

*Nominating*: recommends individuals to serve as officers and trustees, subject to congregational approval

*Personnel*: supervises the synagogue personnel practices code and recommends salaries and benefits for staff

*Public Relations*: promotes a positive image of the congregation among its members and between the congregation and the larger community; assesses membership attitudes toward the congregation

*Religious School*: sets policy and reviews the activities of the schools of the congregation and oversees their operation

*Russian Jewry*: develops programs for awareness and support of individuals and congregations in the former Soviet Union and in other endangered Jewish communities

*Ushers*: trains and provides ushers for religious services and for other functions, as required

*Worship*: works closely with the rabbi; recommends worship innovations and changes

*Youth*: acts as liaison between synagogue youth programs and the board of trustees; recommends and oversees youth programs

# Appendix B

**Survey Form for Synagogue Trustees After One Year on The Board**

## 1. Decision Factors

A. Please indicate how important the following factors were in your decision to accept the nominating committee's invitation to stand for election as a board member.

| | Very Important | Important | Not Very Important | Not At All Important |
|---|---|---|---|---|
| sense of duty | _____ | _____ | _____ | _____ |
| availability | _____ | _____ | _____ | _____ |
| felt ready | _____ | _____ | _____ | _____ |
| inner feelings | _____ | _____ | _____ | _____ |
| need to ensure views represented | _____ | _____ | _____ | _____ |
| strong sense of religious meaning | _____ | _____ | _____ | _____ |
| sense of obligation (to pay the synagogue back) | _____ | _____ | _____ | _____ |
| difficulty saying "no" | _____ | _____ | _____ | _____ |
| service on a community board | _____ | _____ | _____ | _____ |
| desire to change/impact the synagogue | _____ | _____ | _____ | _____ |
| opportunity to be a leader | _____ | _____ | _____ | _____ |
| family involvement in congregation | _____ | _____ | _____ | _____ |
| personal recognition | _____ | _____ | _____ | _____ |

B. Please describe your decision in your own words:

_____

_____

_____

_____

_____

## 2. The Invitation

Please indicate your recollection of the nominating committee's invitation:

|  | Yes | No |
|---|---|---|
| The committee gave me a clear explanation about the duties of the office | _____ | _____ |
| The committee gave me a clear explanation about the religious obligations and implications of the office | _____ | _____ |
| The committee appeared to be simply trying to fill empty slots on the board | _____ | _____ |
| I was encouraged to consider the request slowly and carefully | _____ | _____ |
| The committee wanted me to respond immediately to its request to stand for election | _____ | _____ |
| The committee trivialized the importance of board membership | _____ | _____ |

## 3. Instruction

A. Please indicate whether you believed you needed instruction in the following areas as preparation to be an effective synagogue board member.

When I joined the board I believed I needed instruction in:

|  | Yes | No |
|---|---|---|
| board customs and practices | _____ | _____ |
| the history of the congregation | _____ | _____ |
| the Torah | _____ | _____ |
| synagogue organization | _____ | _____ |
| synagogue documents (bylaws, constitution, etc.) | _____ | _____ |
| organization of the Reform movement | _____ | _____ |
| Reform theology | _____ | _____ |
| order of worship | _____ | _____ |
| liturgy | _____ | _____ |
| goal setting | _____ | _____ |
| conflict resolution | _____ | _____ |
| group-building skills | _____ | _____ |

| | | |
|---|---|---|
| leadership skills | _____ | _____ |
| financial oversight (budget, setting membership fees, etc.) | _____ | _____ |
| staff/volunteer relations | _____ | _____ |
| fund-raising | _____ | _____ |
| speaking or debating skills | _____ | _____ |
| time management | _____ | _____ |

B. Please indicate whether you have received training for your board service in the indicated categories.

After joining the board I received instruction in:

| | Yes | No |
|---|---|---|
| board customs and practices | _____ | _____ |
| the history of the congregation | _____ | _____ |
| the Torah | _____ | _____ |
| synagogue organization | _____ | _____ |
| synagogue documents (bylaws, constitution, etc.) | _____ | _____ |
| organization of the Reform movement | _____ | _____ |
| Reform theology | _____ | _____ |
| order of worship | _____ | _____ |
| liturgy | _____ | _____ |
| goal setting | _____ | _____ |
| conflict resolution | _____ | _____ |
| group-building skills | _____ | _____ |
| leadership skills | _____ | _____ |
| financial oversight (budget, setting membership feeds, etc.) | _____ | _____ |
| staff/volunteer relations | _____ | _____ |
| fund-raising | _____ | _____ |
| speaking or debating skills | _____ | _____ |
| time management | _____ | _____ |

## 4. Preparation

Please indicate what, if anything, you personally did to prepare yourself for board service:

_____

_____

_____

_____

_____

## 5. Behavior

Were any changes in your behavior expected by the congregation as a result of your becoming a board member (e.g., greater attention to religious observance, more frequent attendance at services, greater financial contribution, influencing behavior of your children, etc.)?

_____

_____

_____

_____

_____

## 6. Interest to Serve

A. Were you interviewed by anyone other than the nominating committee to determine your readiness for board membership? Yes/No (please circle)

B. Did you aspire to board membership or consent to it? Aspire/Consent (please circle)

## 7. Installation

How meaningful did you find the board installation ceremony or service?

| | |
|---|---|
| very meaningful | _____ |
| meaningful | _____ |
| somewhat meaningful | _____ |
| only slightly meaningful | _____ |
| not meaningful | _____ |

## 8. Expectations

Please indicate whether or not you had each of the following expectations upon becoming a board member:

| | Expected | Did Not Expect |
|---|---|---|
| close work with the rabbi(s) | _____ | _____ |
| fellowship with other board members | _____ | _____ |
| growth in my faith | _____ | _____ |
| opportunity to share a religious experience with others | _____ | _____ |
| opportunity to solve problems | _____ | _____ |
| opportunity to resolve conflicts | _____ | _____ |
| efficient meetings | _____ | _____ |
| opportunity to support the rabbi | _____ | _____ |
| sense of fulfillment | _____ | _____ |
| opportunity to serve Judaism | _____ | _____ |
| feeling of doing something meaningful | _____ | _____ |

## 9. Orientation Efforts

Please indicate whether or not the following efforts helped you, as a new board member, to feel a real part of the board.

| | Yes | No |
|---|---|---|
| a carefully designed orientation process | _____ | _____ |

|  | Yes | No |
|---|---|---|
| sharing personal and organizational histories | _____ | _____ |
| identification and use of my unique gifts and talents | _____ | _____ |
| assignments relating to my particular interests | _____ | _____ |
| a retreat away from the synagogue | _____ | _____ |
| a goal-setting process | _____ | _____ |
| no effort was made | _____ | _____ |

## 10. Board Meetings

A. Please indicate whether or not, in your opinion, each of the following kinds of activities would help to make a board meeting meaningful:

|  | Yes, Meaningful | No, Not Meaningful |
|---|---|---|
| tackling tough issues | _____ | _____ |
| engaging in Torah study and reflection | _____ | _____ |
| encouraging board members to show respect for all opinions | _____ | _____ |
| reviewing stories of the synagogue and its history | _____ | _____ |
| encouraging everyone to contribute | _____ | _____ |
| sharing personal stories | _____ | _____ |
| singing together | _____ | _____ |
| minimizing dealings with money | _____ | _____ |
| planning for the future | _____ | _____ |
| sharing concerns for one another | _____ | _____ |
| hearing what the rabbi wants | _____ | _____ |
| having the chairperson moderate fairly | _____ | _____ |
| having board members, rabbi, and staff share in decision making | _____ | _____ |
| having rabbi make all significant decisions | _____ | _____ |
| having board members make all significant decisions | _____ | _____ |
| learning about how other congregations solve similar problems | _____ | _____ |

B. Please indicate any other activities that you feel would make board meetings more meaningful:

_____

_____

_____

_____

## 11. Personal Impact

How do you feel your term on the board will affect you personally? Please indicate the strength of your agreement with each of the following statements.

I will:

|  | Strongly Agree | Agree | Disagree | Strongly Disagree |
|---|---|---|---|---|
| gain greater self-confidence in my work outside the board | _____ | _____ | _____ | _____ |
| increase my ability to make tough decisions | _____ | _____ | _____ | _____ |
| learn how groups can come to agreement | _____ | _____ | _____ | _____ |
| gain a greater appreciation of synagogue organization | _____ | _____ | _____ | _____ |
| learn how to embrace diversity within the congregation | _____ | _____ | _____ | _____ |
| gain a greater understanding of how Reform Judaism functions as a movement | _____ | _____ | _____ | _____ |
| learn how to tolerate diversity within the Reform movement | _____ | _____ | _____ | _____ |
| gain greater access to information about Judaism | _____ | _____ | _____ | _____ |
| establish a close relationship with the rabbi | _____ | _____ | _____ | _____ |
| learn how to strengthen my relationship with God | _____ | _____ | _____ | _____ |
| feel burned out, tired and weary | _____ | _____ | _____ | _____ |
| feel enthusiastic about serving on the board | _____ | _____ | _____ | _____ |

## 12. Historical Help

A. Who helps new board members understand how the history of the congregation has a bearing on the board's work and activities? (check each applicable line)

no one; it is assumed that members know rabbi(s)        _____.

administrator        _____.

executive committee members        _____.

other board members        _____.

other:_____        _____.

B. Who gives the most help? How?

_____

_____

_____

_____

_____

_____

## 13. Background Information

A. My age is:

16-25    \_\_\_

26-35    \_\_\_

36-45    \_\_\_

46-55    \_\_\_

56-65    \_\_\_

66-75    \_\_\_

76-85    \_\_\_

B. I am:

female\_\_\_    male\_\_\_

C. The highest level of formal education I have achieved has been:

high school or less       —————

some college       —————

bachelor's degree       —————

master's degree       —————

doctorate       —————

D. Please write briefly about your personal Jewish history (e.g., extent of religious observance, Jewish education, knowledge of Hebrew, length of synagogue membership, service on other Jewish boards, parents' denomination, etc.):

_____

_____

_____

_____

_____

# Appendix C

## What a New Synagogue President Needs to Know

Most congregational presidents function without a job description, and most devise their own orientation programs. The observations below are addressed to newly nominated and newly elected synagogue presidents but are offered only as suggestions, subject to each individual's assessment of institutional needs.

### To the Newly Nominated President-Elect

The first consequence of your new status will be an immediate change in relationships with rabbis, administrative staff, and others. This is not an evaluative statement; it is simply a matter of fact.

An early informal discussion with the rabbi is vital. No matter how closely you have worked with the rabbi in previous congregational roles there is still much to be learned about rabbinic perceptions, objectives, and concerns. To understand fully the role of the rabbi within the congregation and in the broader community will take time and many conversations, but such understanding is necessary if your presidency is to be successful. Try to schedule regular meetings with the rabbi at times and places when you will be free from interruptions.

Experienced administrators have helped congregational presidents start off on the right foot, and any new president would be well advised to sit down promptly with the administrator in order to learn the ropes. As the newly nominated or newly elected president of a congregation, you must take the time to really get to know the administrator and to understand the scope and functions of that office.

Your immediate responsibilities as president-elect will be to begin organizing the new board and to begin planning its agenda for the coming year. Some important preliminaries are as follows.

1. Arrange to receive the synagogue calendar so that you will know about (and attend, when appropriate) synagogue meetings and meetings of other organizations taking place at the synagogue. Arrange to receive the schedules of the rabbi, administrator, and key staff so that you may plan meetings with them.

2. Become involved in decision making that will affect the incoming volunteer leadership team. If a procedure for involving the incoming president in this way is not already in place, develop such a plan shortly after taking office so that the next succession will be made smoother.

3. If you are not already thoroughly familiar with the budget for the period when the new term of office begin, promptly ask to be drawn into budgetary discussions. You and the other incoming officers will have to live with the results.

4. Of greatest importance: develop early working relationships with key officers.

5. Many volunteers express their enthusiasm and their willingness to help. Record these offers so that no one who expresses interest is forgotten when program plans are made and committees are organized.

6. In all this, be sensitive to the feelings of outgoing officers, including the retiring president.

7. Make plans to meet with past presidents to profit from their insights, share ideas, and ensure continuity of leadership. The immediate past president can be of special help in the transition.

Organizing the Board

1. There may be much more enthusiasm displayed by those tapped for leadership positions in a new administration than by at least some of those who are not. Recognizing this, make and announce decisions as rapidly as possible to minimize confusion and ensure continuity of programs.

2. As soon as it is appropriate, meet with the newly nominated officer group to organize the executive committee, plan board committees, and appoint committee chairs.

3. It will be necessary to delegate responsibilities to the vice presidents by clearly assigning specific areas of responsibility to each incoming officer, together with responsibility for oversight of the appropriate committees of the board of trustees. Only in this way will you be free to devote ample time both to sensitive internal matters and to the external contacts which only the president of the congregation can assume. This means working with the vice presidents and others on the executive committee to ensure that the areas to be assigned them are ones of interest to each of them. The board committees for which each vice president will be responsible should be grouped in a sensible way that is understood in broad terms by the board members and the committee chairs who will work with them. In each group, those board committees that require extensive commitment of time should be balanced with others that do not.

4. To prepare for appointing committee chairs, develop a list of prospective chairs in concert with the vice presidents, rabbi, and synagogue administrator.

5. Election of the new board traditionally takes place in the spring, with assumption of office shortly thereafter. It is therefore necessary to give early consideration to planning activities to take place during what is too frequently a summer hiatus.

6. Having announced certain themes and points of programmatic emphasis in your installation remarks, you must make certain that these comments are followed through during meetings of the board of trustees or by other appropriate means.

7. Examine the board-agenda format in terms of expectations of the board members, priority items, matters of Jewish substance, and time limitations on discussion of each agenda item. Consider how to handle reports of auxiliary groups at board meetings, giving opportunity for their leadership to be heard while conserving time for discussion of key agenda items. Assure the administrator a regular place on board agendas and encourage him or her to give a report at each meeting.

8. Develop an agenda for the first meeting of the new board, allowing time for interpreting new board structures and program proposals.

9. Because the president generally serves as chair of the executive committee of the board, plan the agenda for its first meeting. The true role of an executive committee is to act as a sounding board, to funnel committee recommendations to the board of trustees, and to deal with routine matters. The executive committee should not be allowed to make important decisions in which other trustees might feel that they should have participated. The president as executive committee chair must summarize specific items that have been reported to the executive committee for further action, seizing the opportunity to reflect on his or her own recommendations or concerns in vital areas of policy.

Representing the Congregation

1. The congregation should take an interest in regional and national Jewish activities. It should examine the present state of such congregational relationships and prioritize them in terms of importance. The same will be true in terms of other local Jewish and community organizations.

2. Keep informed of the activities of the leadership of area synagogues so

that you may learn from these leaders and collaborate with them when appropriate.

3. Identify means for distributing materials that you receive and designate recipients.

4. Ensure preparation of the synagogue's delegation to significant meetings.

These notes are only a beginning. Each president should add to his or her file and develop a checklist that is germane to his or her own situation. However, the list above will help a new president get organized for the first months of new and sometimes overwhelming responsibilities.

# Appendix D

## Questions a Synagogue President Should Ask After One Year in Office

Generally, the first year of a synagogue presidency is largely devoted to learning the job and understanding the complexity of the organization. The second year presents the president with an opportunity to move the synagogue forward by reassessing ongoing programs and launching new and needed ones.

The first step in this forward movement is the president's self-examination, exemplified in the series of questions outlined below. Every president's questions will be different, as are individuals and synagogues. But the questions should all be jotted down and prioritized so that key issues may be addressed.

Of as much value as the formulation of questions and issues is the opportunity to raise and examine them with the synagogue administrator and rabbi. If the relationship of the president to both the rabbi and administrator has been a good one during the first year, this type of discussion can be productive. It may also encourage the administrator and rabbi to generate their own list of questions.

Often, questions can be divided into three categories: membership services, governing process, and personal development. The questions that follow are offered only as examples. Each president should develop his or her own list in order for the exercise to be meaningful.

Checklist for Membership Services

— Have you set in motion an effort to evaluate membership satisfaction with the various programs of the congregation? Have you taken steps to assess which programs are successful and should be continued, and which are not working well and should be discontinued?

— Do you have a good membership communications program that not only provides information to the congregation on a regular or special basis, but also provides an "effective listening program" to feed back to the leadership the membership's reaction and assessment of programs and services?

— Have you been able to satisfy yourself and your leadership group as to the quality of the synagogue's educational program?

— Have you assured yourself and your leadership group of the quality of the youth program?

— Have you developed programs targeted for such groups as Jews-by-Choice, single parents, or others identified by you as meriting additional programming support?

— Have you examined your congregation's worship program, with particular reference to trends in Reform worship?

— Have you examined the possibility of joint programs with other synagogues in the area?

— Do you have a long-range program that takes into consideration the changing demographics of the community, the aging of the congregational membership, the existence of other synagogues in the area, and so on? Do you know how to develop such a plan or where to turn for assistance?

— Do you have an overall long-term fiscal plan — fund-raising, endowment, legacies, benefits — that will make it possible to minimize dues increases in the future?

Checklist for Governing Process

— Are you satisfied that the size and composition of your board and executive committee are appropriate for making good policy and exercising oversight functions?

— Are you comfortable with the relationship between the board of trustees and the executive committee in the development of congregational policy?

— Have you examined the agenda for meetings of the board of trustees to be sure that the most important items get priority handling? Do board members have an advance opportunity to review background papers or pertinent data in order to make informed decisions?

— Have you developed a balance in the board's agenda so that board members grow Jewishly — for example, in their understanding of worship and educational trends — in addition to discussing organizational and financial matters?

— Does your board of trustees feel a sense of ownership in, and responsibility for, the religious education program even if there is a school committee or a religious school board?

— Have you found ways to integrate the auxiliary units of the congregation — Sisterhood, Brotherhood, Young Couples' Club, and others — into the mainstream of synagogue activities?

— Have you assured yourself that the budget-making process provides the time and mechanism for a careful preparation of the budget and involves the proper officers, committee chairs, rabbi, and administrator at the appropriate time?

— Have you examined the synagogue's staffing to ensure its adequacy, as well to make appropriate use of volunteers, consistent with congregational policy?

— Have you worked out an effective system of communications with the synagogue office so that you receive promptly the information you need and are in a position to act quickly when such action is needed?

— Given that there is no more significant leadership activity than providing for a continuity of leadership, are you satisfied with the procedures, composition, and schedule of your nominating committee?

Personal Development

1. Like it or not, congregational presidents are perceived as role models for the congregation. Have you participated actively in the worship services, or have you become so fatigued from organization and administrative responsibilities that you have absented yourself from Shabbat, festival, or other worship? Have you participated in any educational programs to increase your understanding of Jewish texts, including Reform liturgy, and trends in Reform practice? Have you taken steps to extend your knowledge of the larger Jewish community beyond the congregation?

2. Have you acquainted yourself with relevant publications and electronic communications of the Union of American Hebrew Congregations, Hebrew Union College - Jewish Institute of Religion, and so on?

3. Have you attended a national or regional meeting of the Union of American Hebrew Congregations? If so, have others of your leadership group joined you?

4. Have you established contact with national and local Jewish organizations that can provide resources for your synagogue?

5. Have you made the most of opportunities for extensive, candid conversation with the rabbi and the administrator in order to understand their priorities, sensitivities, and concerns?

6. Are you enjoying your position as president? If not, what can you do in the year ahead to make the experience more enjoyable?

# Appendix E

## Procedure for Self-Study of Congregational Worship

*Purpose*

The purpose of the congregational self-study is to explore the worship experience of the congregation at its most-attended weekly service (probably the late Shabbat evening service).

A self-study is a conversation among a group of congregants about their worship experiences individually and collectively. Decisions about what is important to say about the worship experience lie entirely within the group. The group decides how the conversation should proceed and how it is presented in a final report. The self-study allows the group to decide what they want worship to achieve and to discover whether that is in fact what is happening.

The self-study is designed only to look at the worship experience of congregants. It is not an appropriate instrument for judging any other aspects of congregational life. It is highly inappropriate as a mechanism for evaluating a rabbi, cantor, or educator. But the self-study can be a starting point for discussions within the congregation aimed at making the worship experience more inviting for everyone.

*Method*

A worship self-study team of eight to twelve persons who are representative of the membership of the congregation will worship with the congregation at Shabbat evening services for three consecutive weeks, will keep "worship diaries" about their experiences, and will meet to discuss their experiences and to write a report.

*Leadership*

The rabbi and the president of the congregation will collaborate in selecting the self-study team, in organizing its meetings, and in ensuring the completion of the report. Arrangements must be made for copying materials, as described below. The rabbi may conduct the orientation meeting for the self-study team. The president or another designated person may conduct the subsequent discussion meetings.

The rabbi may be tempted to use these discussions to enhance congregants' understanding of the liturgy. If the rabbi yields to this temptation, the results of the self-study may reflect the rabbi's view of worship and not that of the congregants. For this reason, the rabbi should either avoid attending the team's discussion or deflect questions back to the team for discussion.

Other members of the professional staff should not participate in the self-study. After the team report has been completed, the president will be in a position to help move the discussion of worship and liturgy from the self-study team to the congregation as a whole.

## Selection of the Worship Self-Study Team

Members of the self-study team should be representative of the diversity of the adult membership of the congregation with regard to age, gender, length of membership, attendance at weekly Shabbat services (regular, infrequent, or very seldom) and Hebrew literacy. It may be desirable to include Jews-by-Choice. Team members should be people who are comfortable talking to one another and writing. Beginning with a team of twelve is desirable, since three or four members may unavoidably need to withdraw before the study has been completed. A team of eight to twelve members produces a balanced and lively discussion.

## Orientation

The rabbi will conduct an orientation for members of the team.

It is recommended that each member be given a copy of the "Procedure for Self-Study of Congregational Worship," three "Worship Diary Forms," and a copy of the "Themes for Discussion" (see below).

Each member must clearly understand when, how, and to whom to hand in the diary each week.

At this orientation meeting, members will specify the dates of the three consecutive Shabbat services that they agree to attend. They will also agree to attend two or three discussion meetings after the series of worship services has been completed. Dates for the first two of these discussion meetings should be agreed on at the orientation.

It is important that as many of the team members as possible see the project through to its completion. Otherwise the variety of congregational experiences will be lost.

To initiate their activity, after the first of the worship services the team may be brought together for a half hour, apart from the rest of the congregation, in a small comfortable room where they can begin writing their diaries, or discuss their reactions to the service. Refreshments may be served.

## Use of Worship Diary Forms

Immediately after each of the three services, either at the synagogue or at home, each team member will write a worship diary, using the forms provided and referring to the "Themes for Discussion" as a stimulus to reflection.

The Forms are to be submitted to the rabbi each week for copying and distribution. It is important that the diaries be handled confidentially and copied without attribution of authorship. Copies of all the diaries must be made for each team member, collated in three groups by service dates, and distributed to the team members in advance of the first discussion meeting.

*Discussion meetings*

After all the Forms have been copied, distributed, and read, the team will meet two or three times at approximately weekly intervals for discussion. The length of each meeting should not exceed ninety minutes.

*Recorders*

The team will appoint two recorders to take notes during the meetings. Each of the recorders should note important observations, explanations, suggestions, or sharing of feelings made in the course of the discussions. The recorders should make certain that the group has closed a topic before the discussion proceeds to a different topic. (For example, they might ask, "Have we finished talking about music?") At the beginning of the second and third meetings, the recorders should allow team members to look over their notes on the previous meeting(s) to make additional comments or corrections before discussion resumes.

*Conducting the Discussions*

The discussion leader may commence by introducing a topic from the "Themes for Discussion" and asking what team members have learned about this topic from reading the diaries. Team members are likely to respond by indicating what comments the diaries had in common. The leader may then direct the discussion to the dissimilarities, both from week to week and from diarist to diarist.

The themes need not be discussed in order. As discussion flourishes, the diaries need not always be consulted. The discussion leader should ensure that each person has an opportunity to speak about every topic. If the discussion falters, a more general topic (e.g., how to make worship more effective) may be introduced, or "breakout" groups of three to four persons may each choose a topic, discuss it, and report on it to the reassembled team.

To conclude the discussions the team should try to come to consensus on these questions:

- What makes one worship service different from another, and what parts of the service are most likely to change from week to week?
- How similar are the reactions of congregants to these variations each week?
- How can the worship service be made more meaningful for individuals and the congregation each week? What aspects of the service need to change?

Answering these questions will necessitate analyzing what makes a worship experience effective, and will reflect the variety of experiences of the team members, their differences of opinion, and their most deeply felt spiritual issues. In considering these issues, team members should try to imagine a worship experience that would be meaningful for the entire congregation and to offer concrete suggestions toward this goal.

*Final Report*

The worship self-study team may write its report collectively, using the recorders' notes, or assign the writing of the report to one or two persons.
The report should summarize the team's observations on each of the discussion themes. Every effort should be made to accurately reflect the team's feelings about their worship experiences. The report should conclude with the team's consensus regarding the worship needs of the congregation, its appraisal of congregational worship, and its suggestions for improvement.

The report should be submitted to the president of the congregation and to the rabbi. It may become the starting point for continuing discussion among the congregation and the professional staff of how the worship needs of the congregation can best be met.

**Worship Diary Form**

This diary is for the Shabbat Worship Service on_____

What were you feeling at the beginning of the service tonight?

How did participating in the service make you feel? Did the service work for you? (Discuss the themes of prayer, prayerbook, music, movement, sanctuary, rhythm, Torah study, your life, community, and God, if you wish to do so. Use the other side if necessary. Please write legibly.)

**Themes for Discussion\***

*Prayer*

Prayer is the principal activity of the worship service. Through prayer we attempt to fulfill our spiritual needs, to feel the presence of a community, and to experience the presence of the Deity. Prayer that does all of these things may be hard to accomplish. Think about your praying tonight. Were there some prayers or some moments within prayers that made you feel or think in an extraordinary way?

*Prayerbook*

The prayerbook is the script that enables the congregation to pray together. By repeating the same prayers each Friday night, the order of the service brings the random flow of personal and world events into an orderly pattern. We take the comfort of this pattern with us from the service each week. Think about the words you spoke, either in Hebrew or in English. (Consider transliteration, translations, poetry, language referring to God, order of prayers, etc.) Was there something about the text that enhanced or hindered your experience tonight?

---

\* The characterization of these themes have been drawn in part from Lawrence A. Hoffman, <u>The Art of Public Prayer: Not for Clergy Only</u>, Washington, DC: The Pastoral Press, 1988.

## Music

Music supports our efforts to pray with rhythms that are predictable and melodies that mimic our emotions. Music gives a sense of structure to the service and helps us understand how we should feel at different points. By giving this message to everyone at once, music helps us form a community that virtually "feels together." Did you hear a favorite melody or piece of music at the service tonight? Were there times when you felt the music working to shape your emotions?

## Movement

There is movement during the service, even though most people never leave the space around their seats. At the very least there is sitting and standing, although the traditions of Reform Jewish worship place less importance on moving the body during services than do other Jewish traditions. Movement, like music, supports prayer. How we move helps us express how we feel. Sitting and concentrating, standing and swaying, or respectfully bowing toward the Ark may get our bodies into the worship process. Did movement come easily to you, or were you struggling to make it fit your feelings? How did the movement of others (either those around you or on the bimah) fit with how you were moving and feeling?

## Sanctuary

Prayer takes place in a sanctuary in which the positions of people are predetermined. Did you feel that you were too close or too far away from other congregants or the bimah? At different points in the service, where do you look? When do you close your eyes? What parts of the sanctuary do you look at while you say your prayers? Do you wish you could change some part of the sanctuary layout?

## Rhythm

The rhythm of the worship service changes, depending on the mood of different parts of the service. No two services have exactly the same rhythm. Sometimes recent events in the community, the presence of families marking special occasions, or an impending holiday will influence the rhythm of the service. How would you describe the rhythm of the service tonight? Did the rhythm of the service fit your mood?

## Torah Study

Torah reading may be a significant part of the worship service. A commentary on the Torah portion or a sermon by the rabbi is usual. This part of the service is addressed to us as individuals and as a community. It offers an opportunity for intellectual reflection. How did you respond to the Torah reading and sermon tonight? Did you find a connection between these messages and your life?

## Your Life

When we are praying, we may discover an order to our lives that we were not aware of before beginning to worship. What were you thinking about during the silent meditation? Try to remember all of the times tonight when you thought about the events that happened to you during the week. While thinking about these events, did you come to any new understandings? Were there moments in the service when you were reminded of other times in your life that you felt especially spiritual?

## Community

We worship as a congregation. The ritual of saying prayers together, experiencing the rhythm and music together, moving together in a shared space, sharing the same emotions — all of this together is different from solitary prayer. You may know very little about the lives of the other congregants, about their families, their work, their joys, their sorrows. Still, at the end of the service you knew that you had shared an extraordinary experience together. Did you feel close to the other congregants tonight?

## God

It may be difficult to discuss the presence of God in our worship, to identify the ways in which we envision God. We cannot precisely capture in language our experience of the Divine; but when worship is effective, God is present for the worshiper. Was God present in your worship tonight? Is God ever present for you?

# Notes

Foreword

1. Lawrence Kushner, Memorandum to members of the board of trustees of Congregation Beth El of the Sudbuy River Valley, Sudbury, Mass., 8 September, 1987.

CHAPTER 1

1. "What Do American Jews Believe?" *Commentary*, August 1996, pp. 30-32.

2. Eric Yoffie, Remarks to the executive committee of the board of trustees of the Union of American Hebrew Congregations, 2 February, 1998.

3. Reuven Kimelman, *Tsedakah and Us*, New York: The National Jewish Center for Learning and Leadership [CLAL], 1983, p. 17.

4. Eric Yoffie, "Renewing the Covenant: Our Reform Jewish Future," presidential address to the Sixty-fourth General Assembly, Union of American Hebrew Congregations, Dallas, Tex., November 1997.

5. Neil Gillman, "Judaism and the Search for Spirituality," *Conservative Judaism*, Winter 1985-1986.

CHAPTER 2

1. Daniel Polish, "Commitment in a Reform Context," remarks to the Task Force on Religious Commitment of the Union of American Hebrew Congregations and the Central Conference of American Rabbis, 1987.

2. All quotations from Rabbi Marmur have been selected from his sermons.

3. Peter Knobel, presentation to the Sixty-third General Assembly, Union of American Hebrew Congregations, Atlanta, Ga., 1995.

CHAPTER 3

1. Peter Drucker, "What the Nonprofits Are Teaching Business," *Managing the Future: The 1990's and Beyond*, New York: Truman Talley Books/Plume, 1992, p. 209.

2. Ibid, p. 210.

3. "Trustee Orientation: the Basic Building Block of Board Effectiveness," *Trustee*, September 1992, pp. 12-13.

CHAPTER 5

1. Frank Bruni, "Old-Time Religion with New Twists," *New York Times*, 8 November, 1996.

2. Ibid.

3. "Rabbis for the Twenty-first Century," *Sh'ma*, 21 February, 1997.

CHAPTER 6

1. Study report for the Central Conference of American Rabbis' project on "The Role of Laity in Worship and the Development of Liturgy," August 1995.

2. Mark Washofsky, "Minhag and Halakhah: Toward a Model of Shared Authority on Matters of Ritual," in *Rabbinic-Lay Relations in Jewish Law*, ed. Walter Jacob and Moshe Zemer, Tel Aviv and Pittsburgh, Freehof Institute of Progressive Halakhah: 1993, pp. 99-126.

CHAPTER 9

1. Anthony Ruger, "Financial Affairs," in *Good Stewardship, A Handbook for Seminary Trustees*, ed. Barbara E. Taylor and Malcolm L. Warford, Washington, DC: Association of Governing Boards of Universities and Colleges, 1991, p. 167.

CHAPTER 10

1. "Co-existing with Orthodox Jews," *Journal of Reform Judaism*, Vol. 34, no. 3, Summer, 1987, pp. 61-62.

## Additional Reading

Ashkenas, Ronald N., and Todd D. Jick. *Coping with Change*. New York: Union of American Hebrew Congregations, 1984.

Chait, Richard P., Thomas P. Holland, and Barbara E. Taylor. *The Effective Board of Trustees*. New York: American Council on Education and Macmillan Publishing Company, 1991.

Department of Adult Jewish Growth. *Go and Study: Ongoing Text Study for Congregational Leaders*. New York: Union of American Hebrew Congregations, 1997.

Etzioni, Amitai. *The Spirit of Community: Rights, responsibilities, and the communitarian agenda*. New York: Crown Publishers, 1993.

Greenleaf, Robert K. *Servant Leadership: A Journey into the Nature of Legitimate Power and Greatness*. Mahwah, NJ: Paulist Press, 1991.

Hoffman, Lawrence A. *The Art of Public Prayer: Not for Clergy Only, 2nd Edition*. Woodstock, Vt.: SkyLight Paths, 1999.

Holland, Thomas P., Roger A. Ritvo, and Anthony R. Kovner. *Improving Board Effectiveness, Practical Lessons for Nonprofit Health Organizations*. Chicago: American Hospital, 1997.

Ingram, Richard T., and Associates. *Making Trusteeship Work*. Washington, DC: Association of Governing Boards of Universities and Colleges, 1988.

Lemler, James B. *Trustee Education and the Congregational Board: A Reflection on Leadership in the Community of Faith*. Indianapolis, Ind.: Trustee Leadership Development, 1993.

O'Connell, Brian. *The Board Member's Book, Making A Difference in Voluntary Organizations*. New York: The Foundation Center, 1985.

Olsen, Charles M. *Transforming Church Boards into Communities of Spiritual Leaders*. Washington, DC: The Alban Institute, 1995.

Orlikoff, James E. and Mary K. Totten. *The Trustee Handbook for Health Care Governance*. Chicago: American Hospital Publishing, 1998.

Roof, Ward Clark. *A Generation of Seekers: The Spiritual Journeys of the Baby Boom Generation*. San Francisco: Harper Collins, 1993.

Taylor, Barbara E., and Malcolm L. Warford. *Good Stewardship, A Handbook for Seminary Trustees*. Washington, DC: Association of Governing Boards of Universities and Colleges, 1991.

Umbdenstock, Richard J., Winifred M. Hageman, and Barry S. Bader. *Improving & Evaluating Board Performance: The Complete Guide to Self-Evaluation of the Hospital Governing Board*. Rockville, Md.: Bader & Associates, 1986.

Winer, Mark L., Sanford Seltzer, and Steven J. Schwager. *Leaders of Reform Judaism, A Study of Jewish Identity, Religious Practices and Belief, and Marriage Patterns*. New York: Union of American Hebrew Congregations, 1987.

# About the author

This book is based on Daniel S. Schechter's experience as a synagogue trustee and president, and as a vice chair and executive committee member of the Union of American Hebrew Congregations. He has served as the editor and publisher of *Trustee* magazine, a periodical for hospital governing board members, has written the "From the Boardroom" column in the *Journal of the National Association of Temple Administrators*, and is the author of *Trusteeship in a Great Tradition*, the Union of American Hebrew Congregation's guide for new and prospective synagogue board members. Schechter has chaired the Park Ridge Center for the study of health, faith, and ethics. As codirector, with Rabbi Peter S. Knobel, of the Central Conference of American Rabbis' project on "The Role of Laity in Worship and the Development of Liturgy," he has had the opportunity to observe decision making in many congregations.